# THE CURIOUS
# BARTENDER

## IN PURSUIT OF
# LIQUID PERFECTION

# THE CURIOUS

# BARTENDER

## IN PURSUIT OF
## LIQUID PERFECTION
### RECIPES FOR THE FINEST COCKTAILS

TRISTAN STEPHENSON

WITH PHOTOGRAPHY BY ADDIE CHINN

RYLAND PETERS & SMALL
LONDON • NEW YORK

**Designer** Geoff Borin
**Editors** Nathan Joyce and Julia Charles
**Head of Production** Patricia Harrington
**Picture Manager** Christina Borsi
**Art Director** Leslie Harrington
**Editorial Director** Julia Charles
**Publisher** Cindy Richards

**Prop Stylist** Sarianne Pleasant
**Indexer** Ingrid Lock
**Illustrator** Selina Snow

First published in 2018 as *The Curious Bartender Volume II: The New Testament of Cocktails*; this edition published in 2022 by Ryland Peters & Small
20–21 Jockey's Fields
London WC1R 4BW
and
341 E 116th St
New York NY 10029

www.rylandpeters.com

10 9 8 7 6 5 4 3 2 1

ISBN: 978-1-78879-475-6

A CIP record for this book is available from the British Library.

US Library of Congress CIP data has been applied for.

Printed in China

MIX
Paper | Supporting responsible forestry
FSC® C008047

**A note on sourcing blood for the Claret cocktail on page 196:** when using fresh blood you really need to trust your source and be 100% sure that the product has been packaged under strict sanitary conditions. Fresh blood must be used within 24 hours of slaughter. It's also worth noting that a small amount of blood isn't harmful to your body, but overconsumption (as with most things) can be dangerous.

# CONTENTS

# INTRODUCTION

··········································································································································

*Hello there and welcome to the latest instalment of the Curious Bartender series.
I'm glad you could make it.*

Since *The Curious Bartender: The Artistry & Alchemy of Creating the Perfect Cocktail* was published in 2013, the series has sold over a quarter of a million copies and been translated into multiple languages. Following the success of the first book, I have gone on to write a further four books, which adjusted the focus of the original and took aim at spirits (whisky, gin, rum) and coffee. Although all of these books included a few cocktail recipes, they are mostly works dedicated to specific categories of drink rather than pages of instructions on how to make drinks.

But in the back of my mind I always knew that one day, another cocktail book would need to be written.

To start with, the original book was ready for an update. Trends come and go quickly in this era of craft cocktails and mixology. Drinks ascend into and fall out of favour with the changing of the seasons. Some trends that were the epitome of cool ten years ago now seem crass or just plain boring. That's not to say that the first instalment of this series is not a piece of work I am proud of. It is, in my humble opinion, a fine representation of the slightly awkward adolescent period that bar craft was going through five to ten years ago.

Between 2005 and 2010, the bar industry experienced an incredible period of self-discovery as classic cocktails were revived and new, culinary techniques found their way behind bars. Some of these practices, such as sous vide (see page 38), have, I hope, found a permanent home there. Others, like hydrocolloid caviar pearls, have found themselves homeless.

And then there are the new trends. It's amazing to think that a mere eight years ago you would struggle to find a cocktail bar that carbonated its own beverages on-site. Nowadays, carbonated cocktails are a common feature of bar programs and a whole range of different strategies have been developed to implement them (see pages 57–61). The growing movement towards low- environmental-impact food and drink has led many to take on a locavore approach to cocktail creation

(see Tiger's Milk on pages 80–1) and rediscover traditional preparation and preservation practices such as smoking (see pages 50–51) and fermentation (see pages 43–4), and these techniques have broadened the flavour gamut of mixed drinks. At the cutting edge, liquid nitrogen (see pages 49–50) continues to be as useful for making things cold as it is for extracting flavour from plants, while distilling (see pages 48–9) behind bars has graduated from the status of 'extremely rare' to 'niche'. Perhaps the most radical trend that is currently affecting the bar industry is that of non-alcoholic cocktails. Mixed drinks comprising herbs, juices and sodas littered menus for years, but a new breed of non-alcoholic 'wines', 'spirits' and mixers are taking the bar world by storm and opening up new avenues of alcohol-free mixology (see pages 120–21).

As well as the need to document recent advances, a new cocktail book has also proved to be a good chance to explore a new selection of classic cocktails. This book includes detailed recipes and descriptions for 31 'new' classics that I have not previously explored in my other titles. Most of these drinks were already very familiar to me, but mixing them with a fresh set of eyes and a well-practised palate (that's one way of putting it…) has been extremely rewarding, especially on occasions where I have shared and discussed drinks with the team members at my bars.

Speaking of bars, when I began writing the first *Curious Bartender* title I had just opened my second bar: The Worship Street Whistling Shop. Since then, I have opened a further four bars in London, including a dedicated whisky bar by the name of Black Rock and a sherry bar called Sack. I've also become a restaurateur, opening Surfside – a seafood restaurant in Polzeath, Cornwall. I'm also now the director of a bottled cocktail company, and have more recently branched out into e-commerce with a whisky subscription club called WHISKY-ME.

··········································································································································

All these wider business endeavours mean that these days most of my work is done in front of a laptop screen rather than behind a bar. The slightly unexpected side effect of this change of workplace is that I now spend more time mixing drinks and experimenting with alcohol at home. Most of the classic cocktails in this book have been tested in my home kitchen, and I developed many of the original drinks in this book at home too. This rings true to the ethos of *The Curious Bartender* series, which has always been about building excitement through the exploration of great cocktails and delicious spirits, whether you are an amateur at home or a professional in a bar.

Indeed, this urge to explore, test and create drinks should not be limited to the world's best bartenders. It is something that anyone can do anywhere, and it is my hope that this book can play a role in this creative movement.

Above all, this book is a story about what makes cocktails great and how to go about making great cocktails. It is a book that equips the reader with the knowledge needed to develop original drinks, and perhaps even perfect some of mine. It is a book that links the amateur and the professional as never before. Before you get started, there is just one important precondition that must be met – you have to be curious.

# HOW TO USE THIS BOOK

The first section of this book covers the basic equipment, glassware and ingredients you will need for mixing drinks. You might not need all of this stuff, or you might need all of this stuff plus extra bits that are covered later on. This section is a primer, and essential reading of you're just starting out in the world of cocktails.

The second section covers a wide range of techniques. To begin with, we will take an in-depth look into ice, chilling, and what happens when a cocktail is shaken, stirred or blended. It'll get a bit scientific here, but I can promise you it's worth it and your tongue will thank you for it later. This section also discusses basic taste principles, like sweet, sour and salty. Then we'll look at various preparation techniques in detail, all the way from making infusions through distilling and barrel ageing. It's all there.

The third section of the book is by far the biggest, and this includes all of the cocktail recipes. You will see a flavour map at the start of this section, which plots cocktails according to their alcoholic intensity and how sweet or dry they are. This is a great visual tool for deciding which drink you want to make next, and I personally wouldn't be without it. The cocktails section is organised by base spirit (the main spirit in the cocktail). This isn't the way I would normally organise a cocktail menu, but I've done it this way so that those with only a limited selection of spirits can quickly dial down to those drinks that are within their means. The cocktails themselves are listed in pairs. First comes the classic version of the drink, with all the associated history and commentary, then comes my interpretation of the drink, typically involving more advanced techniques and abstract flavours.

PART I

# THE BASICS

# BASIC EQUIPMENT

There are means and ways of mixing drinks with no equipment whatsoever, but unless you're either a well-practiced bartender or someone who doesn't care about whether a drink tastes good or not (in which case this might not be the right book for you...) this kind of cavalier approach to mixology is best avoided. So you're going to need some equipment.

## JIGGER

The jigger is to the bartender as the knife is to the chef: dependable, always close to hand, and always personal to the individual.

That said, the jigger is really only used to make one or two cocktails at a time, rather than batching large volumes of ingredients, which should be done on a set of scales (see right). The most common type of jigger is made of steel and consists of two cone-shaped measuring vessels joined at the apex. This design gives you two measures for the price of one as well as a way of standing the item on your countertop.

Jiggers come in a whole variety of sizes, which are reflective of imperial and metric measuring conventions and the specific tastes of different nations. Some jiggers also have lines engraved into the inside of them that indicate the level of fill for smaller measurements. Beware of the accuracy of these markings, though, because they have been known to tell lies. It's always worth testing the measurements of your jiggers on a set of accurate digital scales to remove any possibility of doubt.

Scales will also demonstrate what a 'full' jigger looks like – a few millimetres difference in fill height can be the difference between multiple millilitres of volume in the finished drink. This inconvenience is exacerbated by low, stumpy jiggers where a pour that is too high or low results in an even greater error in volume.

Somehow, I managed to get through most of my bartending career with only a 25-ml/50-ml jigger and don't ever recall feeling ill-equipped. But since there are so many jigger models on the market these days, there really isn't any reason (besides cost) not to have a range of measuring options available to you. As a minimum, I would encourage the purchase of a second set that measures 20 ml/40 ml. If you're in the US, you are likely to be more used to measuring in ounces and you may prefer to use a 1-oz./2-oz. jigger. I'll say it now though – and not for the last time – metric measurements are more accurate, and far better suited to scaling recipes up for batching.

## SCALES

Scales are one of the less obvious components of a bartender's arsenal, but they are also one of the most important. Liquids can (and should) be weighed in the same way as solids are, and you'll find weight trumps volume, especially when measuring very small and very large quantities.

With that in mind, it's advisable to buy two sets of scales: one set that is accurate to one-tenth of a gram and therefore good for measuring potent ingredients like powdered acids, hydrocolloids (compounds used to thicken liquids and create jellies, jam and gels) and salt; and another set for batching large volumes, accurate to 1 g and able to weigh up to 5 kg.

## BAR SPOON

Once upon a time, not so long ago, a bar spoon was a barspoon and that was that. Nowadays there is no end to the range of lengths, weights, finishes and aesthetic qualities you can find in the humble bar spoon. All good spoons have one thing in common, though: they're good for stirring drinks. And if I'm honest, that's where there repertoire of tricks should end.

Find a bar spoon that is sufficiently long to fit into a tall mixing glass (30 cm/12 inches is usually long enough) and choose one with a good weight to it so that it sits comfortably in the base of a glass without floating to the top. The actual bowl of the spoon is, quite frankly, abysmal for measuring, but it can be handy for scooping condiments from jars or for taking small measurements of liquid from a mixing beaker for taste testing. The neck of the spoon is typically twisted – a design artefact from bygone days when bar spoons were used to float ingredients – but straight necks are becoming more popular these days. The end of the spoon may have a flat disc on it (for layering), a fork (for picking up things like cherries and olives), a round weight (for cracking ice

cubes), or a simple teardrop shape (for looking pretty). For more about stirring drinks see pages 29–30.

## CITRUS PRESS

You'll not get far in to your cocktail journey without a citrus press close to hand. Don't bother with handheld reamers – they're both messy and inefficient. Instead, get yourself a levered citrus juicer, also known as a Mexican elbow. For more on juicing see pages 40–2.

## SHAKERS & BEAKERS

The primary function of a shaker is to chill cocktails quickly. The secondary function is to keep that cocktail contained and not splattered all over the walls. Barring the cheapest and nastiest examples, pretty much any shaker costing more than £10/$14 will probably meet the above criteria.

So the decision on which type of shaker to buy (broadly speaking, there are three types) becomes a matter of personal preference.

The cobbler shaker (AKA three-piece shaker) is probably what you think of when you close your eyes ad picture a shaker in your head. Although they range in size – from single-serve to comically large – they always consist of a 'tin' (just like a 'tin can', these are in fact made from steel), which is the part that holds everything, a lid with a built-in perforated strainer and a removable cap.

These shakers had fallen out of fashion when I first started bartending, but thanks to the recent renaissance of classic bartending practices brought about mostly by the emergence of Japanese bar culture, they have become popular once again. I like them because they are self-contained units that don't require additional peripherals (you can even use the cap as a jigger), but some people criticise them for being slower and more fiddly than the alternatives.

The Boston shaker is a two-piece arrangement that usually comprises a reinforced 1-pint glass and a 28-oz steel tin (I refer to the imperial measurements here because that's the standard they conform to). Now, you wouldn't think a glass beaker and a metal tin would click together and stay together while being shaken around violently, but they do and it's all thanks to the physics.

When you throw ice in a shaker you're not just chilling the liquid inside the shaker, but the air as well. As the air cools, the pressure drops, which is what keeps the two vessels stuck firmly together. In fact, they can

sometimes become so firmly stuck that it requires quite some effort to separate them again.

The trick to separating them is to hold the large tin with one hand and to hit the top of the tin where the two vessels join with the hard, bony bit at the bottom of your other hand. Boston shakers remain very popular in the US, as well as in bars that tend to serve a high volume of cocktails. This is probably because they have a larger internal volume than cobbler shakers but also because they are inexpensive, almost unbreakable and easy to clean. The downside of this type of shaker is that you need a strainer to go with it.

The third style of shaker is the Parisian. These shakers are a bit of a hybrid between the cobbler and the Boston, although the word 'hybrid' is misleading, as it suggests that it is better in some way. What you actually end up with is a two-piece shaker where one tin slides neatly inside the other but that become nearly impossible to separate after shaking. And while we're at it, I've also noticed a trend towards 'tin on tin' Boston shakers, which suffer from the same sticking problems as the Parisian. The issue with these designs stems from the fact that steel flexes slightly when you press it. Flexibility is actually a good thing when it comes to getting a good, watertight seal. But it becomes problematic when you try and separate the tins using the 'wrist slap' manoeuvre, because both vessels flex on impact and remain firmly stuck.

For stirred drinks, you are more than welcome to use the 'tin' part of any of the above shakers, but I personally opt for a glass beaker with a lip for pouring. Glass mixing beakers have the advantage that you, and the person you are serving the drink to, can see the mixing and chilling of the liquids. This can be handy if you need to correct a drink because it appears to be the wrong colour or has insufficient volume, perhaps because of a forgotten component. From the perspective of a thirsty recipient, it's difficult to measure the impact that stirring in crystal glassware may have on their final appreciation of the cocktail, but it's likely to be a positive one.

## STRAINERS

The purpose of a strainer is to separate a chilled cocktail from the ice that was used to chill it. Even when you're making drinks that are served over ice, it's good practice to use fresh ice cubes, since they will look better and melt slower (see pages 26–8 for more on ice).

There are three types of strainer that bartenders use, plus of course the strainer that you find built into the lid of a cobbler shaker.

The hawthorn strainer is the classic steel strainer that is used in conjunction with a Boston shaker tin. These strainers comprise a metal plate with a handle (mostly useless) and a long spring that serves as a kind of pliable barrier, which allows the strainer sit snugly against the inside of the tin. Then, with your index finger placed securely on top, you can lift the tin and strain with one hand.

The one hand thing is important, because in some instances (see right) you may need to use an additional 'fine' (or 'tea') strainer to remove troublesome flakes of ice. Your spare hand then becomes responsible for holding the fine strainer above the glass.

The third type of strainer – the julep strainer – is to some extent optional, but I quite like to use them when I am preparing stirred drinks. The julep strainer was originally served on top of a julep cocktail (which contains lots of crushed ice and mint) but has subsequently found a better home for itself as a general strainer of stirred drinks.

The relatively large, but sparsely placed holes on a julep strainer make it a poor strainer of shaken drinks, but just about right for drinks that are stirred. Stirred drinks flow more freely than shaken ones on account of the large, uniform cubes of ice and the fact that they don't require the fine filtering of a shaken cocktail. Also, there is a certain elegance in the simple one-piece design of the julep strainer that lends itself well to more discreet preparations.

Depending on the method used to make your drink (shaking or stirring) and the required presentation of the final serve (served over ice or served straight up), I would use the following straining strategies as a basic rule of thumb:

**SHAKEN, SERVED OVER ICE:**
*Hawthorn strainer/cobbler strainer*

**SHAKEN, SERVED STRAIGHT UP:**
*Hawthorn strainer/cobbler strainer + fine strainer*

**STIRRED, SERVED OVER ICE:**
*Julep strainer*

**STIRRED, SERVED STRAIGHT UP:**
*Julep strainer*

# ADVANCED MEASURING EQUIPMENT

Jiggers are great for turning out drinks quickly, but only an amateur would rely on a jigger when developing new drinks or to batch large volumes. For accurate work I would recommend buying a set of plastic, graduated measuring cylinders. Cylinders are cheap, indestructible, and a lot more accurate than a jigger or – perish the thought – a bar spoon. While you're at it, grab a set of plastic syringes too. These are useful for transferring small volumes between vessels quickly, accurately and with minimal mess.

For those of you with unlimited budgets who are really looking to geek out on volumetric measuring equipment, I present to you the micropipette. These little devices are basically souped-up pipettes with a volumetric display that typically ranges from 1–5 ml – great for super accurate measurements of powerful ingredients. As they're intended for laboratory use, you can pretty much name your price on this one, but expect to pay at least £100/$140.

## REFRACTOMETER

Another useful piece of equipment that's finding its way into more and more bars is a refractometer. This piece of kit measures how much light is bent as it passes through a liquid (think the artwork for Pink Floyd's *Dark Side of the Moon*), which is known as its 'refractive index'.

Depending on how the refractometer has been calibrated, the refractive index can tell you things like how much dissolved sugar or salt a liquid contains, or even the alcoholic strength. If you're wondering if this is another extremely expensive piece of lab equipment, the answer is: it can be. It is, however, possible to pick up a perfectly good refractometer for under £20/$28. The important thing to remember with refractometers is that – with the cheap ones, at least – they are only good for performing one task, e.g. measuring the percentage of sugar (or Brix) in a syrup. And as it happens, that's exactly the sort of piece of kit that I would recommend getting. Measuring Brix with a refractometer is the best

(and perhaps the only) way to standardise the sweetness of your homemade syrups and give room to adjust for consistency where necessary. Look for a refractometer calibrated from 0–80°Bx, as this will see you good for even the sweetest of syrups.

There are two important things to remember when using a refractometer to measure Brix. The first is that a Brix measurement tells you what percentage of a substance's total weight is sugar. This means that a sugar syrup of 50°Bx would be equal parts sugar and water, while a syrup of 66°Bx would be two parts sugar to one part water.

The second thing is that a refractometer assumes that there no other substances in your liquid other than sugar and water. This limits the refractometer's use to only syrups that contain little or no salt, and absolutely no alcohol. Liqueurs are off limits, I'm afraid.

## SERVICEWARE

Ok, let's get one thing straight: 90 per cent of cocktails can be served in one of three glasses: the coupe/ Martini glass, the highball glass or the old-fashioned/ rocks glass. Settle on a sensible-sized coupe that can handle both a tiny Martini or a shaken higher-volume drink like a Sidecar. Quantity-wise, 150 ml/5 fl. oz. is usually about right – it won't look like a short serve with 80 ml/2¾ fl. oz. of Vodka Martini in it and it won't be overflowing when mixing a White Lady.

Your highball and old-fashioned glasses will usually be around the same volume, only one will be taller and more narrow (highball) and the other more squat and wider (old-fashioned). Think about what drinks you like to make the most often and consider which size will suit them. I'm a big fan of sticking to a glass that fits the need, rather than shopping around and varying the collection.

All that said, I quite contentedly consume cocktails from tea cups, egg cups or mixed directly back into the bottle. If the drink tastes good, it is good. Serviceware makes it possible to enhance a great-tasting drink but cannot correct the misgivings of a bad one.

It's also contextual. If I'm sipping a Rob Roy on a camping trip in the Scottish Highlands, I'd rather use an enamel camping mug than a crystal Martini glass.

For cocktails served without ice, your glass should always be chilled before use. Serving a cold cocktail in a room-temperature glass is like serving hot food on a cold plate – it becomes impossible to retain the serving temperature. I like to use glasses from the refrigerator for most drinks. These glasses will be at around 1°C/34°F, which is an acceptable level above the common temperature range of most drinks (0°C/32°F to -5°C/23°F). Glasses from the freezer work too (and look cool!), but can often be colder than the cocktail itself, which has the paradoxical effect of making the cold drink seem warm. This effect wears off after a minute or two, though.

Forgotten to put glasses in the fridge (I do)? You can also chill glasses on the fly by adding a few lumps of ice and some water, then quickly stirring for a minute or so.

Taking the time to ensure the glass is at the correct temperature can have a profound effect on your or your guests' drinking experience.

# THIRTEEN BOTTLES

All ingredients are equal, but some are more equal than others. It's true that some cocktails require highly specific brands or styles of drink, but most of the time the exact product you choose won't be of critical importance. It's a common understanding that a cocktail is only as strong as its weakest link, but in reality not all links in the chain are of equal size.

If you're making a Martini, the gin is an important consideration because it is at the forefront of the flavour profile, so care in selection is required. In a cocktail such as the Negroni, where the gin battles against far more powerful flavours than that of dry vermouth in the Martini, there is clearly less need to be fastidious about the brand of gin. Unless you're using a gin with extreme botanicals, or one that tastes bad, in all likelihood your Negroni will taste nice with most brands of gin. I liken it to cooking. If you're making spaghetti bolognese, the cut of minced/ground beef is not as important as the tomatoes, cooking time, pasta quality etc. If you're frying a steak, however, the cut of beef becomes an extremely important factor.

What I'm trying to say here is that in most cases it's all right to select a single brand from each of the main spirit categories and stick with it for the majority of your cocktail making. My main piece of advice when selecting a brand is to make sure you pick one that is versatile, of a premium quality and pleasing to drink neat. For most drinks a generic spirit from the given category will do, but in some instances certain cocktails call for quite specific spirits (you can't put a Navy rum in a Mojito, for example), so I will do my best to point out any drinks where I believe that a specific style, age or brand of liquor is required.

## GIN

More classic cocktails have gin as their base than any other spirit. Indeed, if you were a bartender practising your trade in the 1920s, the vast majority of the drinks you would be asked for would contain gin. For me, gin is all about juniper, so opt for a classic style such as Beefeater or Tanqueray. There are, of course, many newer brands that will also fit the bill.

## RUM

A spirit derived from sugar cane, rum is a key component of many classic punch drinks, most notably those from Cuba and drinks that fall under the category of tiki.

It's difficult to buy a one-size-fits-all bottle of rum, because some drinks call for lighter styles (unaged or lightly aged) typical of the Spanish-speaking Caribbean islands, while others require much heavier styles that you might find in Jamaica or Guyana. A good compromise is a light Barbados or St Lucia rum, such as Doorly's or Chairman's Reserve.

## SCOTCH

A decent blended Scotch is what we're after here and it needn't break the bank. Avoid anything too smoky as this may unbalance the cocktail, and look for fruit and malt characteristics. Johnnie Walker Gold Reserve, Dewar's 12, or Chivas 12 will all do the job fine.

## BOURBON

American whiskey is a staple ingredient of many a pre-Prohibition cocktail. Drinks of that era also used rye whiskey as a base, which takes on a slightly more spicy flavour when compared to the slick sweetness of bourbon's higher corn content.

A good compromise is Woodford Reserve or Bulleit, both of them bourbons that contain a healthy measure of rye in the mash bills (the mix of grains used).

## COGNAC

French brandy was the original mixing spirit in the mid-19th century, and it remains a fantastically versatile cocktail ingredient. A good VSOP (Very Superior Old Pale) from any of the major Cognac houses will work perfectly well, though if you want my recommendation I would suggest looking at Pierre Ferrand.

## TEQUILA

The golden rule when buying tequila is to only buy a bottle that says '100 per cent agave' on the label. If it doesn't say '100 per cent agave', it means the spirit contains some corn or wheat-based distillate, which serves to boost the alcohol content and dilute the natural vegetal flavours of the plant upon which the drink should be based. Aged tequila can taste quite different from the unaged stuff, so to cover all bases I suggest buying a *reposado* ('rested') which will have been aged for between two and 12 months.

## VODKA

Let's not sugarcoat it – nine times out of ten it's difficult to discern the difference in a vodka once it's been mixed into a cocktail. That one time, however, such as when you mix a Vodka Martini or a Vesper, will demand a decent liquid, so on that occasion, it's worth buying something you'd be happy to sip on. My recommendation is for a rye vodka like Belvedere or Vestal, or a potato vodka like Chase.

## TRIPLE SEC

Triple sec (meaning 'extra dry' in French) is similar to Curaçao, which has its origins in the Dutch Caribbean island by the same name. Both are orange liqueurs made from the peel of bitter oranges, but Curaçao tends to be sweeter. I would recommend a triple sec such as Cointreau, and the recipes I provide are based on a spirit of that sweetness.

## AMARI

Bitter aperitifs like Campari or Aperol are fantastic ingredients to keep around because they make delicious long cocktails like the Americano. They are also as the chief component of the legendary Negroni cocktail.

## VERMOUTH

If you're looking for a one-bottle solution to vermouth I suggest plumping for a bianco style, which is light in colour but still rather sweet. If your budget can stretch to two bottles, get one extra-dry (French style) and one sweet, aka *rosso* (Italian-style). Always store vermouth in the fridge and aim to finish the bottle within 30 days. **Tip** – mix it with soda and ice for a delicious alternative to a white-wine spritzer.

## ABSINTHE

Contrary to what you might have heard (or perhaps experienced), absinthe is not the hallucination-inducing poison that it is sometimes labelled as. It is typically quite high in alcohol (this is to stop the liquid from looking cloudy as it contains oils that fall out of solution in low-alcohol conditions) but is not designed to be consumed neat. Absinthe is best consumed with plenty of ice-cold water, or in such classic cocktails as the Sazerac and Corpse Reviver No. 2. The best brands are those produced by Jade, as well as Butterfly and La Clandestine.

## MARASCHINO

This cherry-flavoured liqueur is arguably just as important as triple sec in the field of cocktail modification. It became popular around the same time as its orange counterpart. Maraschino has miraculous mixing powers, and the ability to pull a poor-tasting drink out of a nosedive. Luxardo is the go-to brand here.

## DRY AMONTILLADO SHERRY

Yes, I am a bit of a sherry fiend, but it's also my belief that a small drop of sherry will have the effect of improving virtually any cocktail it comes into contact with. It often works well in place of vermouth too, and there are great classic cocktails such as the Sherry Cobbler that rely on sherry as the base ingredient.

# KITCHEN INGREDIENTS

Unless you're content with cocktails made entirely from booze (which can be nice sometimes), you're going to need a basic catalogue of kitchen ingredients. Now, there's a good chance you're holding stock of this stuff already, but it's worth taking the time to check before embarking upon an evening's cocktail making.

## SUGAR

Caster sugar is a staple product that can easily be converted into sugar syrups for cocktails, or as a base for flavoured syrups. You may wish to experiment with darker sugars too, such as demerara and muscovado – these work very well in cocktails that call for aged rum.

## SALT

Salt performs a similar role in mixed drinks as it does in food, elevating flavour and softening bitterness, sweetness and acidity. Cocktails rarely taste salty, but a touch of salt will improve most drinks. Keep table salt for making syrups and infusions, and flaked sea salt for rimming glassware and garnishing.

## SODAS

It may sound simple, but keeping a good stock of sodas can be a bit of a challenge, as they tend to lose their fizz quite quickly. This is something that you can let slide when it's just a glass of fizz you're after, but a G&T without the bubbles is a sorry affair, just as a Mojito without that lick of spritz can also feel a bit flat.

Soda water, tonic water, ginger beer and cola make up the four pillars of your carbonated world.

## HERBS

Fresh herbs can be used as visually attractive and aromatically pleasing garnishes as well as components of the cocktail. Fresh herbs can be tricky to store, though. Too much moisture can make the leaves go slimy, and too little moisture makes them dry out, while excessive light turns them yellow. Store soft herbs like mint, coriander/ cilantro and basil in the fridge, but arrange them like a bunch of flowers in a glass jar with water in the bottom. Woody herbs like rosemary, thyme and sage should also be refrigerated, but last longer when wrapped in damp kitchen towel and placed in a sealable container.

## HONEY

A great modifier that can be used in place of sugar syrup in almost any cocktail, assuming you like the flavour of honey, of course. Honey plays especially well with grain-based spirits like gin, vodka and whisky.

## MAPLE SYRUP

Similarly to honey, maple syrup can add a buttery, candied note to mixed drinks, and works rather well with American whiskey.

## AGAVE NECTAR

Disproven as a health food it might be – but you're not drinking Margaritas because they're healthy, right? – agave nectar certainly has a strong affinity with agave spirits (tequila, mezcal) as well as cachaça and agricole rums.

## EGGS

The use of eggs, egg yolks and egg whites in cocktails has a long history. Many old-fashioned drinks like flips, possets and syllabubs require a whole egg to add both flavour and texture to a drink. Lots of cocktails that emerged from the golden era of mixed drinks (1860– 1930) also call for egg white.

## CITRUS FRUITS
See page 35.

PART II

# TECHNIQUES

# INTRODUCTION TO CHILLING

All of the liquids on a bar store heat energy, and when you mix them with ice, an energy tug of war starts and it doesn't finish until the last gram of ice melts. As the battle unfolds, the liquid chills, the ice melts, and at some point along the way you get a cocktail that is sufficiently cold and not overly diluted. But for the super-curious among you, there's a lot more detail to be explored here.

## HOW CHILLING WORKS

The chilling of a cocktail occurs by two physical processes that take place simultaneously. The first is the direct conduction of heat from the liquid to the ice. In other words, the liquid gets colder because the ice is cold. Turns out that it takes 209 joules of energy to warm 100 g/3½ oz. ice up by 1°C/34°F (this is known as the specific heat of ice), and that energy is 'stolen' from the liquid in the form of heat, resulting in a colder drink.

Of course, this exchange of energy only works so long as the cocktail is warmer than the ice cube, and ice normally melts at the same temperature it freezes at: 0°C/32°F. But most cocktails are served at subzero temperatures, and some drinks may be as cold as -10°C/14°F. This low temperature is achievable because alcohol–and–water mixtures have lower freezing points than water. Nonetheless, how can the 0°C/32°F surface of a melting ice cube chill a drink below 0°C/32°F?

The clue was in the question: melting. While it takes just a paltry 209 joules of energy to warm 100 g/3½ oz. of ice by 1°C/34°F, it takes a whopping 33,400 joules of energy to melt 100 g/3½ oz. of ice into 100 g/3½ oz. water. This is known as the heat of fusion of ice. Just like in the specific heat process, the energy needed to melt the ice cube is drawn from the heat of the liquid, which subsequently chills the cocktail.

In fact, the vast majority of the chilling power of an ice cube comes from melting, not the fact that it is cold. You can conduct a simple test to prove this point by freezing some large pebbles and comparing their chilling power to an equal weight of ice. Put the ice in one glass and the frozen stones in another, then pour over a spirit of your choosing and stir for a minute. The pebble drink will be noticeably warmer on your lips. The reason? Pebbles don't melt.

If you attempt this test with water, you'll find that the temperature never drops below 0°C/32°F no matter how much ice you use. At 0°C/32°F the ice and water reach a state of equilibrium, where the energy needed to melt the ice is balanced by the ice cubes' resistance to melting. Things stay the same, sort of (see below).

In cocktails, things work differently because alcohol–and–water mixtures have a lower freezing point. The temperature of a Martini, for instance, continues to lower as you stir below zero and the ice continues to melt. This is because the drink still has heat energy, despite being cold. That energy, particularly when coupled with stirring or shaking, is enough to melt the surface of the ice even though both the drink and the ice are chilled below zero. The drink continues to get colder until it approaches its freezing point and a state of equilibrium.

## THE OVER-DILUTION MYTH

Introducing too much dilution into a drink was a worry that loomed heavily over the generation of bartenders that I come from. We were taught to pour the drink into the glass as soon as stirring or shaking had finished, to avoid ongoing dilution of the drink. Turns out this is a poor strategy. Science has since taught us that very little dilution occurs after a cocktail has been mixed and once it has reached equilibrium, and here's why.

Once a cocktail nears its freezing point, the chilling begins to slow and eventually plateaus. This is because the drink cannot get any colder while remaining in a liquid state. Following this logic, a drink with a static temperature is a drink that is retaining all of its heat energy. And since you can't melt ice without heat, the ice in your shaker or mixing beaker stops melting. Nearly.

At this point, ice and cocktail join forces and pick a fight with every joule of thermal energy. Most notable of these, is the surrounding, presumably warm air, the glassware or shaker, and your hands. Rather than warm up, the ice continues to melt (slowly) to maintain equilibrium while the drink dilutes, decreasing its ABV and increasing its lowest potential liquid temperature. In the end the drink finds its way back to room temperature. Unless you drink it first, of course!

## ICE IN COCKTAILS

If you're one of the people reading this book who makes cocktails at home, you probably don't have the luxury of a £3,000/$4,000 Hoshizaki or Kold Draft ice machine. It's a sad fact that bagged store-bought ice is universally composed of small hollow lumps that are invariably broken down into smaller non-uniform pieces. In a fix, it will do OK for shaking cocktails, but it's barely satisfactory for stirring drinks and totally unacceptable for a finished serve. It's far better, and cheaper, to make your own ice. In fact, I recommend dedicating a single freezer drawer to this noble practice.

There are dozens of ice-mould options available on the internet these days. If you're making ice at home you will need to get a good stock of trays that make 3-cm/ 1-inch cubes. This will be the ice you use for shaking and stirring all of your cocktails, so you're going to need a lot of it. Get in the habit of making and storing ice so that when you really need it there's tons of it there.

Whether making ice in a bar or at home, you should also consider getting moulds that make large 5-cm/ 2-inch cubes. These look great presented in a rocks glass and can even be trimmed down to spheres using an ice pick. You might prefer to buy a mould that produces perfect spheres, but I find perfect spheres in drinks a bit too… perfect, and would sooner have a craggy-looking lump any day of the week.

If you want to make the best presentation ice, though, I wouldn't bother buying any moulds at all. Crystal clear ice can be made in a home freezer; it just takes a bit of planning, time and patience. It's definitely worth the effort, though, as you will see from some of the cocktails pictured in this book.

## MAKING CLEAR ICE

Ice goes cloudy when impurities and dissolved gases in the water cause ice crystals to break their uniform structure and form gas-filled imperfections in the cube or block. Commercial ice manufacturers get around this with machines that turn hundreds of litres of water into massive blocks that freeze from the bottom while stirring the water on top. This has the effect of concentrating all of the dissolved gas, dust and minerals in the liquid on top and leaving only perfect ice underneath. Nature performs a similar feat when a lake freezes, only this time the ice freezes from the top down, since it's the cold air that is causing it to freeze in the first place.

The best approach for making clear ice at home is to recreate the conditions of a lake (no fish required).

This can be achieved with an insulated cool box, which gets filled with water and popped inside your freezer. It's best to boil and then cool the water before using it, and filtered water is preferable over tap/faucet or mineral water. Because the sides and bottom of the box are insulated, the ice freezes from the top down, pushing most of the impurities to the bottom of the box.

The trick is to pull the box out of the freezer before the bottom 20 per cent of the water freezes, which can take anywhere from two to four days depending on the size of your cool box. Once you have disposed of the unfrozen liquid, you can give yourself a good pat on the back – you just made clear ice! If you took your cool box out too late, don't worry. You can simply cut off the cloudy end of the block.

## CUTTING ICE

I recommend three pieces of equipment for handling block ice: a long, serrated knife, a wooden mallet and an ice pick – no, not the kind of ice pick you might go mountaineering with, but the kind of handheld pick with one or three spikes on the end that's used to chip away at blocks of ice. This is one tool that can't be substituted easily with another kitchen implement, so it's worth investing in.

Ten years ago, I was rather adept at transforming a large chunk of ice into an imperfect sphere (think moon-shaped) in under a minute. I'm very much out of practice now though, and therein lies the secret. The trick (as if it needs explaining) is to carefully and methodically trim all of the corners and edges off the cube. The very best ice carvers can achieve this with little wasted ice and no wasted movements.

The knife and mallet are good for breaking down large blocks into more manageable-sized chunks. It's always best to let big blocks of ice warm up for a while once you take them out of the freezer. As with ice cream, this tempering process softens the ice slightly and makes it easier to cut into uniform shapes.

Position the ice on a non-slip surface (a damp tea towel or a bar mat work well for this), then use the serrated blade to score lines into the block. Now tap the mallet on the back of the blade to split the block. In my bars we have a dedicated ice saw for this process, but they're rather specialist. Ours *might* have been smuggled back from Japan.

# SHAKING & STIRRING

An iced drink that is sitting still will get colder, but it will take quite some time. This is because a static liquid has only limited contact with the ice, so heat becomes unevenly distributed. Melted ice sticks to the surface of the ice cube and hinders further melting, while a few millimetres away (near the edge of the glass, for instance), the drink is warmer. To facilitate further chilling, the cocktail has to rely on the lower temperature of the adjacent ice-hugging liquid to slowly leach heat energy from the rest of the liquid in the glass. I like to compare it to a large party where everybody's feet are stuck to the ground and only the guests surrounding the buffet tables get fed.

Whether it's stirring or shaking, mixing improves the efficiency of the chilling process.

## SHAKING

Shaking a drink is almost the quickest practical pathway to cold cocktails (see Blending on page 30). The first reason for this is the rapid distribution of liquid around the shaker and amongst the ice. This increases the surface contact area of liquid with ice and speeds up the exchange of heat between the two components. It also means the faster you shake, the faster you chill. There's another reason why shaking chills quickly, and that's because the ice cracks and breaks apart, increasing the overall surface area of ice along the way.

In general, a shaken cocktail's temperature will reach equilibrium after less than ten seconds of shaking. Shaking any longer than that will have very little further effect on temperature or dilution of the cocktail. Shaken drinks are also aerated to some degree, because the action of whipping up the cocktail with ice causes air bubbles to become trapped in the liquid for a time. We are able to detect these tiny bubbles on the palate, and in some cases they can profoundly affect the tactile experience of the cocktail and the way in which we perceive flavour.

The Japanese bar scene has contributed a number of great things to Western bartending over the past few years. The most useful of all is the wide selection of quality barware and tools.

Another significant influence that has come out of Japan has made a lot of Western bartenders reconsider the way in which they shake. When I first heard about the 'Japanese hard shake' I assumed it was a way of shaking a drink hard (makes sense), but if anything it should refer to how hard it is to master.

The aim is to bounce the ice off every surface of the shaker by moving the shaker in a highly specific pattern. It looks a lot like a dance step but with a cocktail shaker. The intended result is a drink that, quite simply, tastes better. The pioneer of the technique, Kazuo Uyeda of Tender Bar in Tokyo, is adamant that the drink is better in every way, but in tests that I have conducted myself, the pattern in which you shake (provided that it's not excessively slow) makes no measurable difference to the temperature or dilution of the cocktail.

So, once again, science wins over.

That leaves only the element of aeration. Sadly, measuring aeration and viscosity is much harder to do and requires in-depth qualitative testing to truly determine whether the hard shake really does make a better drink.

## STIRRING

The most important thing to understand about stirring is that it takes rather a long time to get to really low temperatures. When stirring, the ice and the cocktail interact more slowly than they do when shaking, so you have to do it for longer. A lot longer, in fact. In tests that I have conducted, it takes at least 90 seconds to stir a couple of Martinis to the same temperature as a ten-second shake.

Now, you can be forgiven for assuming that a drink stirred for 90 seconds will become more diluted; after all, the liquid is in contact with the ice for longer – and ice melts! That last bit is true, but what's also true is that ice can't melt without heat. Heat is taken from the drink, chilling it down. Whether stirred, shaken, or built in the glass, the physics are always the same: there is no chilling without dilution and no dilution without chilling.

The temperature and dilution of the cocktail are relative – only the time it takes to get there changes.

## SURFACE AREA

Mixing a drink is one way of increasing the surface contact area between cocktail and ice. The other way is to increase the surface area of the ice itself. And the most obvious way of doing this is to use more ice. More ice means a larger surface area, plus you're increasing the overall size of your heat-draining resource, meaning you can potentially chill a larger volume of liquid, too. Another way to increase the rate of chilling is to use smaller cubes of ice, or better still crushed or flaked ice. Smaller pieces of ice have a larger surface area to volume ratio, so drinks made with crushed ice will often reach a satisfactory temperature in a matter of seconds.

The shape and size of the ice you use to mix your drinks makes virtually no difference to the final temperature and dilution of the cocktail (there is one caveat to this – see below). Whether it's crushed, cubed or even big rocks of hand-cracked ice, they all eventually achieve the same level of dilution and temperature. Surface area is, again, relative to time. Lower the surface area and you increase the chilling time.

So small chips of ice are best then? Not necessarily. The problem with crushed ice is that it tends to be wet (bear with me). Ice always melts from the outside in, and if left to sit around, a thin film of water quickly melts onto the surface of the ice. On ice cubes this is bad, but on crushed ice it can be disastrous, on account of the high surface area of the ice. A large surface area means more surface water. When added to the cocktail, the water on the ice will immediately dilute the drink. This creates a kind of feedback loop, as that immediate dilution also means it becomes harder for the ice to do its chilling job since it has more overall liquid to contend with. The (now larger) drink calls upon further ice meltage to facilitate chilling, which creates even more liquid volume.

It's a cruel chain of events that, as a bartender, is certainly best to avoid. My advice is to use re-frozen ice, or drain away the surface water by running it through a salad spinner (or swinging it around in a cloth bag) before use – you'll be surprised how much water hides in all those nooks and crannies!

The problem with the oh-so-fashionable chunks of hand-cracked ice is that their low surface area will negatively impact the time it takes to stir a cocktail to an acceptably low temperature. Spheres are the worst for this, because a sphere has the lowest surface-area-to-volume ratio of any three-dimensional shape, plus a single large sphere tends to just rotate on a vertical axis when stirred in a mixing beaker. This makes for an extremely inefficient chilling process, which might never reach an acceptably low temperature. So, save your big lumps of ice for finished serves.

## WHAT'S THE BEST ICE TO USE IN THE COCKTAIL?

Despite a strong argument for large lumps of hand-cracked ice in a finished drink, it's also important not to let head rule over heart.

Some drinks are inseparably intertwined with iconic visual appeal and when constructing these serves, great care must be taken not to pervert the history that has brought them to our recipe books today. For example, drinks like the Rum Swizzle (see pages 144–5) generally call for crushed ice – partly due to its speedy cooling capacity, but also because the ice plays a big part in the presentation of the drink too.

If you have ever been served a Mojito with cubed ice, you'll have noticed that the mint clumps together and likely floats near the top of the drink. Crushed ice allows the bartender to encapsulate the mint leaves of the drink within layers of frozen nuggets, evenly distributed through the glass, changing the visual impact from that of a stagnant pond to a perfectly layered, icy, mint-infused glacier.

Likewise, the tropical connotations that are implied by crushed ice have no place in the seductive leather-embossed, cigar-smoking ritual that surrounds a cocktail such as the Rusty Nail (see pages 154–5).

For an Old Fashioned, a single lump of hand-cracked ice perfectly reflects the quiet contemplation that should accompany the drink.

## BLENDING

Since surface area is the biggest deciding factor with regard to the rate at which a drink chills, it should come as no surprise that a blender is the most efficient form of chilling available. A good blender can transform ice and liquor into a dozen head-achingly cold slushy cocktails in less than ten seconds.

Unlike straight up and served-over-ice cocktails, a blended drink is suspended by tiny particles of ice. And whether you're drinking through a straw, with a spoon or just taking big mouthfuls of the drink, you will inevitably ingest all of the ice in a blended drink through the course of its consumption. I tend to blend cocktails with about one-and-a-half times as much ice by weight to achieve the right (slushy) texture. That's quite a lot of dilution of flavour in every mouthful, so you'll need to compensate by making a reasonably potent cocktail in the first place.

It's also worth remembering that sweetness becomes more suppressed as a drink gets colder, so if you're converting a classic recipe to a blended spec, it's often necessary to up the sugar.

## MATERIALS

This section would not be complete without a quick note on materials. It's only recently that I have taken a much stronger interest in the materials that I use to stir and shake drinks, and how they affect temperature and dilution. Early test results have shown huge differences in drink temperature and the associated dilution based on the thermal conductivity and thermal mass of the shaker or mixing beaker. I envisage a time in the not-too-distant future where we select specific equipment for specific drinks based on the target temperature and dilution of that drink.

Just like ice and booze, the material that a shaker or mixing beaker is made from stores energy that has the potential to melt ice. The difference with the ice melt here, as opposed to that which we have already discussed, is that it will not contribute to the chilling of the drink but instead, the chilling of the shaker/beaker. The trick, then, is to a choose a beaker or shaker that limits dilution as much as possible (if you want a little more dilution in your cocktail you can always add water before mixing).

Thinner materials have less thermal mass than thicker ones, so a good starting point is to use thin-walled shakers and beakers. That usually means picking a metal shaker over a glass one, since glass becomes fragile when it is thin. The problem with most metals, however, is that they have quite a high thermal conductivity. That is to say, they warm up and cool down with relative ease. Some materials, like plastic and styrofoam are famously poor conductors of heat, which is why they are sometimes used as insulators for cool boxes or refrigerators.

So the ultimate solution to all this is to use a lightweight shaker made from a low-conductivity material. This naturally leads us to plastic, which, while not the most attractive type of shaker material (nor does ice make the same satisfying sound as when it is shaken in a metal shaker) is the best commonly available material used to make shakers that you can buy.

Another option is to use a heavy shaker or beaker with a high thermal conductivity that has been chilled in a freezer. This material will act like a heat sink for your cocktail, sucking up energy into its large stores of thermal mass and actively assisting with the chilling process. So pop a heavy-glass mixing beaker in your freezer drawer.

# SUGAR & SYRUPS

There's only one drink in this book that contains no sugar at all, and that's the Bullshot (see pages 88–9). All of the rest are sweetened, whether through the use of granulated sugar, honey, some other sweet condiment, or by way of a liqueur, cordial or vermouth. Sugar plays an important role in cocktails, and is particularly good at accentuating floral, fruity and herbal characteristics in drinks, and providing body and length to a cocktail that errs on the lighter side.

When I use sugar, I tend to use sugar syrup. There are only a handful of occasions where I would advise using granulated sugar instead of a syrup, and that tends to be when making a drink that has a muddled fruit component. Granulated sugar works like an exfoliant on fruit skins and can draw out a pleasant zesty quality in cocktails such as a Ti Punch, which uses whole chunks of lime, or Old Fashioned, which calls for muddled orange zest. Of course you could make a flavoured syrup by blending the zests with sugar and water and then straining through a muslin/cheesecloth, but some drinks are not quite the same when we forgo the rituals that have become synonymous with them (even if quicker and more consistent methods of production are available).

I make sugar syrup by mixing two parts of sugar by weight with one part of water by weight (I call this 2:1 syrup and it's this sugar syrup that I refer to throughout this book). Just pop them in a saucepan over a low heat for a few minutes, stirring until the mixture turns clear and the sugar has totally dissolved. If you're making sugar syrup for the first time, you may be surprised to find that a mixture containing twice as much sugar than water will eventually form a fluid syrup, but it does.

Some bartenders prefer to make their syrups to a ratio of one part sugar to one part water (1:1 syrup). This naturally results in a less sweet syrup, though not half as sweet as 2:1 syrup, as the numbers might initially suggest. A 25-ml/¾-fl. oz. jigger of 2:1 sugar syrup contains 16.6 g sucrose, whereas 25 ml/¾-fl. oz. of 1:1 sugar syrup contains 12.5 g sucrose, so the 2:1 syrup is actually 33 per cent sweeter. To put it another way, if you are making a recipe that calls for 10 ml/⅓ fl. oz. of 2:1 syrup you would need to use 15 ml/½ fl. oz. of 1:1 syrup. I uses 2:1 because it keeps better (sugar is a natural preservative) and because it limits the amount of additional water I am adding to my cocktails.

All sugar syrups should be stored in the fridge and will become mouldy if left unrefrigerated for too long. If you're intending on using your sugar syrup only for alcoholic cocktails, you might consider adding some vodka to your recipe. A sugar syrup with an ABV of just 5 per cent will keep for roughly twice as long as one with no alcohol in it. To make a 2:1 alco-syrup of 5 per cent ABV, simply replace 20 per cent of the water in your recipe with vodka (do this after mixing, while the syrup is cooling).

Unless otherwise stated, all of my syrups are made from caster sugar, which is 100 per cent sucrose. Sucrose is itself formed from one molecule of glucose joined to one molecule of fructose. Most sugars are pretty bad for you but fructose has one of the highest glycaemic indexes and is directly linked to type 2 diabetes. It's also rather difficult to avoid.

All of the sweeteners mentioned on page 22 also comprise equal parts fructose and glucose (honey) or are primarily sucrose with a little glucose and fructose mixed in (maple syrup), with the exception being agave nectar, which is primarily made from fructose and is therefore the least healthy of all the commonly used cocktail sweeteners. Honey, maple syrup and agave all tend to be between 70–80 per cent sugar by weight, so a little sweeter than 2:1 syrup.

Low-calorie and calorie-free sweeteners are not products that I generally use in my bars. This is because there's a trade off to be had between flavour and points on the glycaemic index. In some instances, the residual flavours of alternative sugars can contribute positive characteristics to a drink, such as the nutty flavour of rice malt syrup. In other instances, such as with stevia and xylitol, those secondary flavours are harder to integrate or cover up.

You can turn virtually any ingredient into a syrup by extracting its flavour in o water, straining, then sweetening. The various strategies for creating infusions detailed on pages 37–9 will serve you well for this.

# SEASONING COCKTAILS

Seasoning a cocktail is not something that we normally think necessary to do. In the kitchen, salt, acids and umami flavours are commonly used to add depth and breadth to a dish. So how do we do it in cocktails?

## SALT

Salt, in the correct quantity is universally recognised to improve flavour. I have personally introduced salt to more and more of my creations over the last few years, for the simple fact that they taste better with a pinch of salt. Salt suppresses the perception of bitterness and astringency, and as with food, it is highly effective in accentuating the positive characteristics of a drink. The important distinction to make here, though, is that in most cases the salt shouldn't be noticeable. For me that means keeping the usage down to around 0.25–0.7 per cent of the total weight of the drink.

Traditionally, alkaline salts have been used in the production of selzer water and soft drinks as an acidity buffer. Salt has the effect of softening acidity slightly, and as such has been used to soften the slightly nasty carbonic acid present within carbonated water. It is also used in the production of acid phosphate, a traditional acidulent for flavoured sodas, made by adding salts to phosphoric acid.

I tend to mostly use classic sea-salt (sodium chloride) flakes. They are easy to handle, highly soluble and good for extracting flavours when left to infuse with dry ingredients (e.g. flavoured salt). There are naturally salty alternatives to salt, though. Bacon is becoming a commonly used salty ingredient as either a fat wash – the process of mixing rendered fat with a liquid then allowing it to stabilise and filtering it back out – or infused directly into spirits and liqueurs.

Soy sauce, miso and fish sauce both have a reasonably high salinity too, but use carefully and be aware of the style before chucking it straight into a drink! Shrimp paste has salty/sweet characteristics – the first time I was served shrimp paste in a Bloody Mary I was blown away by the flavour.

It's becoming quite common for bars to keep a dasher bottle of saline solution behind the bar, which can be called for on those occasions when a cocktail is lacking a certain something to balance it and integrate flavour. Simply mix (by weight) one part salt with ten parts water and store in a bitters bottle or a bottle with a pipette.

## ACID

Bartenders have historically used lemons and limes as souring agents. They do a very good job of balancing sweetness and adding a 'fruity' flavour to the drink. Acid is important in many drinks, as a certain tartness activates the salivary glands on the side of your tongue, resulting in loads of nice saliva to swish the drink around your mouth. There are plenty of alternatives to citrus fruit, though, and in many cases these other ingredients can be very cost-effective too.

### CITRUS

The obvious choice for many a bartender. Citrus is natural, stores reasonably well and provides theatrical and aromatic effect when freshly squeezed into a drink.

Lime tends to have a lower pH than lemon (1.8 versus 2.3) but both have a concentration of around 5 per cent pure acid. Lime comprises both citric and ascorbic acid, whereas lemon is almost entirely citric acid. Orange and grapefruit have a similar pH of around 3.7 (oranges have more sugar in them, so feel less sour).

Personally I prefer citrus juice freshly pressed and I think this is partly due to the minimal oxidation of the aromatic oils that make their way into the juice from the peel. Others suggest that a few hours resting improves the juice, but everyone agrees that lemon and lime juices need to be used on the same day that they are juiced.

### PURE ACIDS

The cheapest, easiest and least romantic way to use acids is to simply purchase them in their pure, powdered form. I used to use a pH-testing kit to dilute my acids down, but later discovered that it was pointless because it bears little relevance to how acidic things actually tasted. This is because the tongue detects the concentration of acid in a solution, rather than the pH (which refers to the number of free hydrogen ions). The upshot of this is that it's best to just taste acids, mix them in cocktails and work to an acceptable level of sourness. The good news is that most of the organic acids listed below have a similar weight of acidic molecules, so can be interchanged with one another quite easily.

**Acetic acid** – Found in vinegar. One of the few acids that has an aromatic quality to it. Present in shrubs and useful for seasoning savoury cocktails (if that's your thing). More on this below.

**Ascorbic acid** – Pure vitamin C, which means it's naturally present in most fruits and vegetables. Crisp and bright tasting.

**Citric acid** – Found in citrus fruit, especially lemon. Bright, sharp and clean… a bit like lemon, really.

**Lactic acid** – Found in dairy products and fermented products. Tastes of burnt milk, sour cream, buttermilk and various fermented items like sauerkraut.

**Malic acid** – The acid found in green apples and nectarines. It's fruity, bright, crisp and has a longer linger than most other acids.

**Tartaric acid** – Found in grapes. Pretty darn sour.

## OTHER FRUIT

There are various fruity alternatives to our skin-clad, segmented citrus friends. Some of them may be sourced locally to you and so tick boxes where provenance, sustainability and reducing food miles are concerned. Below is a brief rundown of the predominant acids present in common fruits. Note that many of the fruits below contain other acids in trace amounts, but I have only listed detectable acids in the table.

## VINEGARS

As used in shrubs, vinegar might sound like a strange choice, but in the right quantities or when coupled with citrus juice it can add amazing depth. Vinegar contains acetic acid and the intensity of the acidity does tend to vary according to style. Some vinegars, such as balsamic, have significantly more flavour than others and this is something to bear in mind when using them.

| FRUIT | Citric acid | Malic acid | Tartaric acid | Oxalic acid |
|---|---|---|---|---|
| Apple | | ✓ | | |
| Blueberry | ✓ | | | |
| Cherry | ✓ | | | |
| Cranberry | ✓ | ✓ | | |
| Currant | ✓ | | ✓ | |
| Gooseberry | ✓ | | | |
| Grape | | ✓ | ✓ | |
| Kiwi | ✓ | | | |
| Lemon | ✓ | | | |
| Lime | ✓ | ✓ | | |
| Nectarine | | ✓ | | |
| Orange | ✓ | | | |
| Passionfruit | | ✓ | | |
| Peach | | ✓ | | |
| Pear | | ✓ | | |
| Pineapple | ✓ | | | |
| Rhubarb | ✓ | ✓ | | ✓ |
| Strawberry | | ✓ | | |
| Tomato | ✓ | ✓ | | |

# INFUSIONS & EXTRACTION

Manufacturing liquors, bitters, cordials and tinctures has become a staple part of bar craft in recent years. While the classicist's approach requires very little in the way of homemade ingredients, any budding bartender, whether amateur or professional, who is committed to making awesome drinks, must be comfortable with the idea of making awesome ingredients too. The production of these ingredients can all be classified under the heading Infusions.

The advantage of pre-infusing liquids is that the product can be stored and reused with confidence in its consistency. Making a redcurrant liqueur, for example, will yield better long-term results and require less time overall than 'muddling' redcurrants and sugar every time you wish to make a drink.

There are a number of techniques that can be used to introduce flavour into spirits or to create water-based infusions. Alcohol and water are both good solvents and do an excellent job of drawing out and suspending the volatile compounds of the ingredients that they come into to contact with. Infusing and extracting these compounds is the basis for the production of many flavoured spirits and liqueurs.

## FUNDAMENTALS

In its simplest form, an infusion is affected by the size of the particle(s) to be infused, the weight of the particle(s), the temperature, pressure and alcohol content.

It's generally accepted that chopping something to half its size will make it infuse four times faster. This has not only a huge effect on the time it takes to infuse a liquid, but often the amount of spice, herb or fruit that you need to use. So long as the particles are not so small that you cannot filter them out afterwards (see Clarification on pages 46–8), it is almost always better to chop or grind ingredients as finely as you possibly can.

Density and intensity are much harder to measure than size. A pink peppercorn is far more intense of flavour and dense of structure than a white tea leaf, for example. All ingredients are different and it would need a lot of pages to list the relevant infusion times and quantities for every single commonly used ingredient. In this book I recommend weighing ingredients and

scaling them according to the quantity of infusion required. For example, for a vanilla-flavoured vodka, you need only infuse 3 per cent vanilla where the vodka is 100 per cent (i.e. 3 g per 100 g vodka) for 24 hours at room temperature.

The aim is to infuse the ingredient at the right pressure and temperature for a length of time that best extracts all that is good about the ingredient without extracting bad, astringent or bitter notes (unless bitterness is what you're after!).

Warm infusions speed up the extraction process of almost everything, as well as extracting solubles that are unobtainable at lower temperatures. In its simplest form, a warm infusion is a pan and hob/stove. For many ingredients this is the quickest and most efficient infusion process, and excellent when making flavoured syrups and liqueurs, because sugar can be dissolved while the solution is still warm. The downside is the potential for heat-based spoilage. Fruit zests begin to stew at sustained high temperatures, herbs release undesirable bitter chlorophyll notes and the subtleties of flowers are overpowered by generic vegetal characteristics.

## MACERATION

The most common form of infusion is simple maceration: adding herbs, spices, nuts or fruit, usually to water (usually with sugar) or alcohol. Macerations can be either cold or warm, depending on the product you're infusing; they can also take anything from an hour to many years to get the best results.

Speak to any bartender and almost all of them will admit to their first foray into infusion being a bottle of vodka, a herb or fruit of some kind, and a warm coffee machine or glass-washer.

Despite all the modern practices used for infusing flavours, a bottle of liquor with some herbs chucked in still remains a very effective and cheap way of doing things. This is partly due to the fact that the technique sucessfully 'contains' the infusion. Think about it —when a chef makes a tasty stock and fills the room with a wonderful aroma, all that aroma is flavour lost from the stock itself. Keeping flavour sealed in is one of the key steps to a successful infusion.

## SOUS VIDE

Sous vide is a precisely controlled method of warm maceration. The process has two main benefits: the prevention of the loss of volatile aromatics during the cooking process, and the precise control of temperature.

It works by sealing ingredients into plastic pouches, then cooking them in a water bath. This technique is used widely in modern kitchens as a way of precisely cooking meat and vegetables, but it's also a fantastic way of extracting flavours into water and alcohol. Sous vide has some great advantages when it comes to making homemade cocktail components: the precise control of both temperature and time of infusion; even distribution of heat throughout the infusion; no risk of burning or overcooking; and a sealed package, meaning that no aromatics can escape.

Sous vide is a technique that involves pouring liquid (the 'infuser') and solid (the 'infusee') ingredients into a heat-resistant plastic pouch, or ziplock bag. Your infusion is then placed in a heated recirculating water bath, set to a precise temperature.

The exact temperature will vary depending on what kind of product you are infusing and which section of the product's flavour spectrum you are looking to extract, but it will generally sit between 50–90°C/122–195°F.

The length of time required will also differ from one ingredient to the next, but marvelling at how many different iterations of flavour can be taken from one ingredient by adjusting time and temperature is part of the fun of sous vide. It's best not to worry too much about the ratio of 'infuser' to 'infusee' too much and always use as much 'infusee' as you can. This way, you're making a concentrate that you can dilute back with more water/alcohol afterwards, reducing the number of times you need to make more infusions.

The trend now seems to be toward sous vide circulators, which are compact devices that can sit on the edge of any container and circulate warm water around. You simply set the temperature and let it do its thing. Quickly going out of fashion (on account of their size, which is fixed and generally quite large) is the all-in-one water bath. At a push, you can use a pan of water on a stove with a thermometer stuck in it, and carefully adjust the hob to maintain a stable temperature.

You can buy inexpensive counter-top vacuum packers for less than £100/$140 nowadays, but I wouldn't bother. The counter-top sealers work by drawing a vacuum out of the pouch, which inevitably draws your liquid out too unless you get the timing of the heat sealer absolutely spot on.

Chamber vacuum packers negate this issue because they depressurise the entire inside of the chamber before forming a seal, so the contents of the bag simply bubble (as the boiling point inside gets lower) and the bag compresses once the chamber is pressurised again. The problem with chamber vacuum packers is they cost over £1,000/$1,400 and they're big.

The best solution for infusing drinks is actually the cheapest – ziplock bags. Removing the air from a ziplock bag is really easy, and you can do this by partially submerging the open bag in the water bath, and sealing the 'zip' once all of the air is displaced out of the bag. Ziplocks are also reusable, so you only need to buy them once and never need throw away any plastic.

## PRESSURE INFUSION

Infusing ingredients under pressure can speed up infusion time significantly. You can do this using a pressure cooker. Pressure cookers are essentially large pots with a pressure-sealable lid. They are excellent for infusions that require a decent amount of heat in order to best extract flavours, because pressure cookers work by increasing the boiling point inside the cooker.

Most pressure cookers have a gauge that indicates the pressure inside the device. Add water and some hardy spices that enjoy high temperatures (burdock root, star anise, sarsaparilla, for example). At 15 psi/1 bar of pressure, the water inside a pressure cooker will boil at 120°C/250°F, extracting flavours that wouldn't be obtainable without this increased temperature. **Warning**: Never pressure-cook alcohol-based infusions, since high temperatures and alcohol vapour are not safe together!

## RAPID NITRO INFUSION

Another simple and inexpensive method that relies on pressure as a means of extraction is 'nitrogen cavitation'. This method calls for a iSi cream whipper or siphon that uses 8-g $N_2O$ canisters.

It involves adding liquid and solid matters to the cream whipper, charging it with one or two cartridges, waiting for a few minutes, then rapidly ventilating the gas from the cream whipper, and finally filtering your infusion. You should shake or wiggle your infusion while it is taking place to dissolve the gas into the liquid. This forces the liquid to infuse into the solid matter. When you release the pressure quickly, the

nitrogen builds in the liquid, forming explosive bubbles that create enormous turbulence, speeding up the infusion time. Repeating this process a few times can yield incredible results in just a matter of minutes.

One of the huge advantages of nitrogen cavitation is that the infusion doesn't require any heating and, therefore, the ingredients aren't susceptible to temperature-based spoilage. Perhaps the biggest disadvantage is the relative cost of the gas cartridges compared to the basically cost-free alternative of a long, cold maceration. I've also found that nitro infusions are far better at extracting light, floral and fruity top notes as opposed to rich earthiness, spice and bitterness.

Nitro infusions work best with porous, solid ingredients, such as spices, roots, barks and some dried fruits. Fresh fruits and vegetables have evolved natural defence mechanisms in their physical structures that prevents this kind of infusion being effective. Cutting them up can sometimes overcome this.

To get maximum pressure into your infusions, it's best to fill your whipper to the recommended maximum fill line (which tends to be either 500 ml or 1 litre). This leaves less headspace in the whipper, which increases air pressure and forces more nitrogen into your solution. Larger whippers tend to need two blasts of a cartridge.

Even though the headspace left in a fully filled whipper tends to be about the same across all whipper sizes, there's more liquid in a bigger whipper, so you need more gas to fill it to a similar pressure.

# JUICING & DRYING

The ability to juice fruit and veg effectively and in an appropriate manner to their physical structure is extremely important for mixing drinks. Extracting juice from a fruit may seem like a simple thing. After all, in its most basic form it requires only a squeeze of the fingers to liberate the complex nectar from an orange. But some fruits require specialist treatment, occasionally in unconventional ways, to best access their flowing juices.

This all starts with respect. Fresh fruit juice contains a cacophony of complex volatile oils, lipids, protein, acids and sugars. Retaining the best bits is vital in the quest for delicious drinks. Having said that, almost all juicing techniques require a not-insubstantial level of violence.

## PRESS

A press can constitute anything from a handheld citrus press (called a Mexican elbow) to a heavy cast-iron (often bolted down) lever-operated press. Either way, the premise is simple. Crush the fruit enough and the cells will rupture, releasing the juice to fall through a mesh or coarse filter to be collected below. These devices work really well for citrus fruit and perform badly with everything else.

The concave bowl of a levered citrus press suggests placing the fruit skin-side down and pressing the dome of the juicer through the soft tissue. This is in fact not the most efficient way to use a citrus press. You're far better off placing the fruit in there skin-side up, then forcing the dome through the skin, causing the fruit to turn inside out and extracting maximum juice.

## JUICER

Juice extractors come in two varieties: the first is the fast-spinning kind, which are basically centrifugal graters that separate juice from pulp by way of gravity and mesh filters. Centrifugal juicers are fast and cheap but you tend to lose a fair bit of liquid in the discarded pulp. The second kind of juicer, which works a lot like a mincer, is a masticating juicer. These devices comprise a slow-spinning corkscrew (known as an auger) that forces the fruit or vegetable through a filter, dropping fresh juice out of the bottom and dry pulp out of the end. Masticating juicers tend to be more expensive and slower, but they are extremely efficient, meaning that very little juice gets wasted.

Whichever machine you opt for, it will work very well for ingredients that have a high water content but are reluctant to let go of it, such as carrot, celery and apple. A good juicer can even extract liquid from things that seem to have no liquid, like ginger, sweet potato and even nuts! The only downside of a juicer? Cleaning. That's why it's best to juice a lot in one go and consider freezing or preserving juice for a later date. If you freeze your juices into ice-cube trays, they can be used to shake or build cocktails that will never suffer from overdilution!

You can pick up a good centrifugal juicer for very little money, and while they do the job fine, they're useless for large quantities and bits tend to snap off easily. If you fancy investing in something more substantial, I recommend Omega and Champion as solid brands that can take a beating. Both start at around £350/$500.

## FREEZE JUICING

It might seem counter-intuitive to freeze fruit in the pursuit of extracting juice from it, but the technique works very well for soft fruit. Freezing a blackberry causes ice crystals to form in the cell structure of the fruit. The cells then rupture, and once the fruit is defrosted the juice will flow much more readily when processed through a juicer. Repeated freezing and defrosting will yield even better results.

## ENZYMATIC JUICING

Chemistry can be an excellent assistant in the pursuit of free-running juice. Many of the proteins that make up the structures of fruit and vegetables also have 'anti-proteins' or enzymes that break apart the mortar that holds the brickwork of the plant together. The structure of an apple, for example, is held together largely by pectin (the same stuff that jam and marmalade makers use to harden conserves). Soaking the sliced fruit in a pectinase solution will soften the fruit considerably, thus making extraction of juice that little bit easier.

## OSMOTIC JUICING

If your goal is fruit juice for the production of a syrup or liqueur, osmotic juicing is for you! It works on the principle that water inside the juice will always try to equalise with its surroundings, a process known as osmotic pressure. Sprinkling sugar all over strawberries and allowing them to rest for a day or so will cause much of the juice to leach out as it attempts to moisten the surface of the fruit. Following that, simply juice as normal – the resulting juice will be obviously be sweeter than without the sugar treatment.

# DRYING

Drying ingredients might seem like a strange thing to do in the goal for tasty cocktails – after all, you can't drink something with no liquid in it! As true as that statement is, there is a place for dried and powdered ingredients in the creation of delicious drinks.

For millennia humans have stored ingredients in low-humidity environments to encourage the desiccation of water and the preservation of the food. Dried herbs and dried fruit are two of the most common dried goods that we encounter on a daily basis – everything from a pot of oregano to a raisin undergoes a drying process, but why? Well, firstly it vastly extends the lifespan of the product, and secondly it concentrates the flavour. Removing the water from a fresh apricot means that there is a higher concentration of all the flavourful compounds present within the fruit left behind. Dried food can then be used to infuse flavour, powdered down and turned into a sherbet, or simply used as a decorative garnish.

There are some very expensive ways to desiccate and dehydrate food, most of which are used in commercial applications such as the production of instant coffee. Some of these processes involve blasting thin jets of liquid with warm air; others involve slowly thawing frozen ingredients under low pressure. It's more likely that you would use an inexpensive cabinet dehydrator, or simply an oven or hairdryer!

Dehydrating ingredients by heating them with warm air works by evaporating the water in the product and lowering the humidity around the product (let's use a slice of apple as an example). The heat causes the water on the outside of the apple to evaporate away, raising the ambient humidity. Constant airflow lowers the humidity, and moisture from within the apple migrates to the surface, continuing the evaporation cycle. Dehydrating with warm air typically takes place between 35–80°C/95–175°F (warmer air will usually dehydrate

more quickly). The one caveat with this is the process of case-hardening, where the temperature is too high and the exterior of the product dries hard, preventing further water from evaporating. Case-hardening is exactly what happens when you bake bread. Low and slow is nearly always the best strategy for drying ingredients when complete desiccation is the goal.

## POWDERED LIQUID

Since drying liquids into a powder is very difficult without expensive equipment, I have navigated around this by first mixing the liquid with sugar. Icing/confectioners' sugar works very well, because it contains a small amount of cornflour/cornstarch, which helps with thickening the liquid. Combine the liquid (spirit or otherwise) with icing/confectioners' sugar, then paste it onto perforated greaseproof paper and place in the dehydrator at 40°C/105°F for 12 hours (or a low oven) and you'll be left with a thin sheet of flavoured sugar. Grind the sugar up with a pestle and mortar, or put it through a coffee mill, and the powder can be used for dusting drinks, or for flavoured sugar rims.

You can also try the same process with salt, which could result in some interesting salt rims for Margaritas.

## DEHYDRATED GARNISHES

Drying garnishes can result in stronger aromas, visual appeal and powerful tastes. Even something as simple as a slice of lemon can look amazing once dehydrated. The added bonus being that it will keep just fine for many weeks afterwards in an airtight container.

I have found that dehydrated ingredients impart much more flavour into cocktails than their moist counterparts. A dehydrated banana slice in a Daiquiri releases much more flavour into a drink than a slice of fresh banana. This is because the dried product becomes hydroscopic (absorbent) once dehydrated, which allows the flow of liquid in and out of the cracks and capillaries of the fruit, thus increasing infusion time significantly.

## INFUSION

As with above, infusing flavour into your syrups, liqueurs and cordials is often a lot easier and more economical with dried products. Moisture in fruit and vegetables acts as a protective layer, preventing access from the outside without crushing, cutting or heating. Remove the water and you have unlimited access to the inner flavourful structure of the plant. It's also that a much lower weight of the product is required for a desirable outcome.

# FERMENTATION

Fermentation can cover a whole host of topics related to the production of drinks and alcoholic beverages. Indeed, all of the drinks in this book (with the exception of the non-alcoholic First Aid Kit – see pages 120–1) rely on fermentation of a sugar or starch to bring them into a state of existence that permits optional distillation and subsequent mixing into a cocktail.

This section is not intended to discuss spirits and wine production as such, but to address the growing trend for low-alcohol fermented tonic beverages that are becoming prevalent in the world's top bars.

Besides basic baking-yeast fermentations of ginger beer and root beer, fermented tonics include a broad family of fermented products, each made from a particular culture of yeast and/or bacteria and each being built from a specific substrate or material. There are fruit juice-based ferments like *tepache* and *aluá* that hail from Central America, root-based sweet potato and cassava ferments from South America and the bread-based ferment *kvas* from Russia. There is also the kefir family of drinks, which use a versatile yeast/bacteria culture that has the appearance of white clumped balls, and the super-trendy kombucha (see page 44) that is the result of sweetened tea fermented using a gelatinous disc otherwise known as a SCOBY (symbiotic culture of bacteria and yeast).

All of these fermentations share some commonality (a good balance of sweet and sour, rumoured health-giving properties, a slight effervescence), yet each produces a unique style of drink, and this is something that requires consideration based on the material you are fermenting and the desired outcome.

Fermentations can be used in cocktails in place of fruit mixers, where they contribute a flavoursome lactic sourness that can complement fresh, herbal and grassy flavours. They can also stand alone as mixers for spirits, taking the place of tonic water or ginger beer. A good fermentation can also be a great stand-alone drink that requires no mixing whatsoever.

Perhaps the most important rule of fermentation is cleanliness. Since you will be creating the perfect conditions for yeast and bacteria cultures to thrive in, you will need to ensure that the ones that do grow come from the intentional propagation rather than infection. Boiling water and sterilising tablets are your friends here, and be sure to give the same treatment to any utensils that may come into contact with your ferment.

This is an especially important rule of 100 per cent yeast- based fermentations, where bacteria is undesirable and will ruin the fermentation. You can be less fastidious with cleaning when making things like kombucha and kefir because the liquid is being purposely inoculated with a massive bacterial culture that will protect the fermentation from the incubation of other cultures.

## APPLICATIONS OF FERMENTATION

In most applications of fermentation you will want to store your product in a warm environment (20°–24°C/68–75°F) with as little as possible natural light (UV light kills yeast and bacteria cells). The time a fermentation takes is relative to the temperature. This is why it can take weeks to brew a batch of kombucha in the winter but only a matter of days in the summer.

Fermentations involving 100 per cent yeast (like my Banana Barrel Whisky Mac recipe – see pages 168–9) tend to work best in a closed environment that prevents contaminants from infecting your brew, and limiting the availability of oxygen during a brew improves yeast efficiency. Fermentation produces $CO_2$ (see below), however, and this needs ventilating to avoid a build up of pressure and, potentially, an explosion. With small-scale ferments this is usually done using an inexpensive airlock valve that sits on top of your bucket/carboy/demijon/barrel. For yeast ferments, standard brewer's yeast usually works just fine. It's also fun to explore yeast strains that are traditionally used for certain types beer or wine, like Champagne yeast, for example.

As you might expect, these yeasts will steer a fermentation in a similar direction (in terms of flavour, fizz and potential alcoholic strength) as the wine or beer they are associated with.

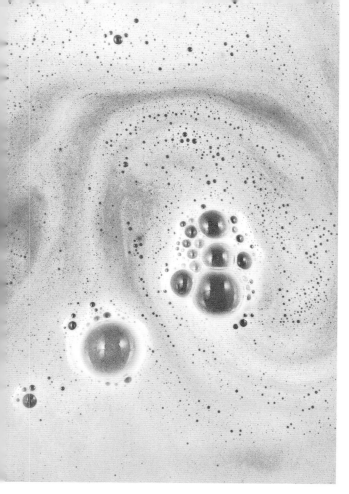

## KEFIR AND KOMBUCHA

For kefir and kombucha ferments, oxygen isn't such a problem since the end game is not the production of alcohol but the development of sourness and bite.

I tend produce these ferments in 2-litre wide-mouthed jars covered with cloth and a rubber band. When making either of these products you will need to acquire a SCOBY (kefir SCOBY are often referred to as 'grains', although by definition they are also a type of SCOBY) to get you started, which will allow you build a stock of culture.

## CARBONATION BY FERMENTATION

Before pressurised $CO_2$ became the go-to method for soft-drink carbonation, all drinks were carbonated by natural fermentation.

Ferments from open vessels (like kombucha or kefir) may be slightly effervescent if they are highly active, but insane (potentially dangerous – see below) levels of carbonation can be achieved by popping your ferment into a sealed bottle. This needs to be done while the ferment is still active and there are still unfermented sugars in the brew. Once in a sealed bottle, the yeast will continue to create $CO_2$, but with nowhere for it to go, it dissolves in to the liquid. Depending on your desired level of fizz, sometimes only a few hours are required, other times it may take a couple of days. The trick is to refrigerate your ferment to deactivate the yeast before the bottle explodes.

If you wish, you may also add a little extra sugar to your ferment when bottling (known as 'priming') so that the yeast has material with which to create $CO_2$. This can also help with bolstering the residual sugar content of your finished product in situations where most of the sugar in the fermentation is already depleted.

Gauging at what point enough fizz has been made is the tricky part: too short and your finished product may lack fizz and be overly sweet; too long and you risk an explosion, or a drink that foams violently when you open it and that is insufficiently sweet. Practice makes perfect.

The risk of explosions is why I like to bottle at least some of my fermentation batches in plastic bottles with screw caps. A quick squeeze of the bottle gives some indication of how much pressure is inside – you can use a shop-bought bottle of soda for comparison. The good thing about using plastic for some bottles is that there's then nothing to stop you bottling the rest in flip-top glass bottles or even with crimp caps like you find on beer bottles. You can use your plastic bottles as a barometer, and glass bottles for presentation.

Remember that glass bottles have the allure of looking more authentic, though nothing screams amateur like fragments of broken glass in your hand.

# FILTERING

I've covered the basic strainers for mixing cocktails (see pages 16–17), but you'll need a broader range of filtering devices for preparing infusions and creating ingredients.

A large chinois is a good place to start, both in terms of a first purchase, as well as where pretty much any form of filtering is concerned. The holes are big enough to not get clogged up easily and you can fit a lot of liquid into a chinois, which while being good if you, say, have a lot of liquid, also applies downward pressure on the liquid passing through the filter, speeding up the process.

A muslin/cheesecloth will take your filtering to the next level in terms of clarity. There aren't many solids that will make it past a muslin/cheesecloth and they're both cheap and reusable (make sure you keep your muslin/cheesecloth clean). It pairs well with your chinois too, where you can simply line the chinois with muslin/cheesecloth and filter as usual.

If a muslin/cheesecloth isn't sufficient for your filtering needs, the next step might be a Superbag. These bags are quite expensive for what is in fact just a bag, but they are pretty good at what they're intended to be good for: filtering. Superbags can be up to 8 litres/8½ quarts in size and have very fine apertures ranging from 250 to 50 microns in diameter, the latter being just one twentieth of a millimetre.

As a final resort, you can always turn to paper filters. A coffee filter will work just fine for this, but make sure you choose a large one, because filtering through paper can be painfully slow. Paper also has the effect of trapping many of the oils that may be present in your liquid. This can have either a positive or negative affect on the aromatic quality of your product as well as its mouthfeel. If you want to get an idea of the real-world difference a paper filter makes, try brewing coffee through paper and cloth and tasting the difference.

# BLENDING

Blenders have been a common sight on back bars for decades now, but I personally find that I very rarely look to a blender for assistance. True, there are some drinks that should be blended (Piña Colada, Batida, Frozen Daiquiri) and obviously a blender is useful for their production, but grinding spices and making purées is about where it ends from a ingredient-preparation point of view.

Vitamix and Blendtec are the best-known and best brands in the blending world. Both are capable of incredible feats of chopping up and turning things into powder. It's actually quite incredible the abuse that these machines can take, as proven by Blendtec's 'Will it Blend' series of YouTube videos.

The Vitamix has the edge on functionality because it has a speed-control knob. This is essential if you want to avoid splattering your ingredients all over the side of the blender jug and continually stopping, scraping down the sides, then starting again. The Blendtec is like an untamed beast in this respect… but golly, does that thing blend.

If you can afford it, a better investment than a blender is a Thermomix. Part blender, part stove, part scales; these space-age gadgets are in virtually every Michelin-starred kitchen on the planet and many of the world's best bars too.

I love them because they can gently stir or totally annihilate a mixture while steadily holding a temperature. You can even spin the blades backwards, which turns your Thermomix into a surprisingly effective ice-crusher (most blenders are terrible at crushing ice and produce a kind of snow instead). Granted, the £1,000/$1,400 price tag is enough to put most people off, but when you consider the range of abilities that this piece of kit has under its belt, the expense really does become justifiable.

# CLARIFICATION & CENTRIFUGE

Whether it's removing a stubborn cloudy haze or transforming an opaque drink into one that is crystal clear, clarification can be very handy if your aim is a 'purer' looking cocktail or you just want to confuse someone by making their Margarita look like water! Cloudiness is caused by insoluble particles that are suspended in your cocktail. Their insolubility is the root of the problem, because it causes light to bounce about the place, which gives the drink an opaque appearance. But insolubility is also to our benefit. By being that little bit detached from the drink itself, these particles leave themselves open to extraction!

There are a whole bunch of ways to clarify liquids, covering a variety of budgets and levels of technical involvement. Old-school mesh/sieve filtering should always be your first stop, since it's cheap and easy and will remove large lumps of insolubles. Beyond that, you have the various gel-clarification methods that I have listed below, enzymatic clarification, purpose-built electric filtering equipment, and – for hardcore clarifiers – centrifugal separation.

## RACKING

Those of you with little patience can take a pass on this section. Racking not the most exciting method of clarifying a liquid, but it can be highly effective if you have the time and inclination to wait. It tends to work best on liquids that have quite large insoluble particles and that don't contain stabilisers (whether natural or otherwise) that prevent movement of materials around the vessel.

## GEL FILTRATION

Gel filtration is a method of clarification that uses gelling agents to trap insoluble particles in a 3D organic mesh, separating them from clear, flavoursome liquid. When I first discovered this technique, I used gelatine to clarify orange juice. The process involved gently heating the orange juice, whisking gelatine into the juice, then letting the jelly set in the fridge (if that sounds a lot like making a jelly, that's because it is). Next, you put the jelly in the freezer until solid, then take it out of the freezer, wrap it in muslin/cheesecloth, and allow it to defrost at room temperature for a few hours. The shock of freezing and then thawing the jelly causes most of the liquid in the gel to leach out, and it can then be captured and used to make your cocktail. The stuff that's left in the muslin is a kind of slushy gunk that holds on to all the insoluble particles.

The whole process was extremely time-consuming and barely worth it for all the effort involved. Fortunately, someone came up with the idea of using an alternative gelling agent that could achieve what gelatine does in under an hour. Ladies and gentlemen, allow me to present you – agar.

Agar is extracted from red algae. It makes a more brittle jelly than gelatine, which you wouldn't generally want on your dessert plate, but has the benefit of being vegetarian-friendly. For clarification purposes it is vastly superior, however.

The first difference between gelatine and agar gels is that agar doesn't technically require any refrigeration to set and will do it just fine at room temperature. The flip side of this is that it does need dissolving at a higher temperature than gelatine. In fact, you will need to nearly boil the liquid you're clarifying to properly activate agar. This is a drawback, since nine times out of ten this method will be used to clarify fruit and vegetable juices, which will spoil at high temperatures.

The best way around this is to boil only a small portion (20 per cent of the total liquid, for example), then add 2 g agar per 1 kg of total liquid. Whisk the agar in and then temper the rest of the cool juice into the gel solution. Allow the solution to set in an ice bath (not essential but good for speeding things up) and it should quickly form a loose gel. Gently break up the gel using a whisk and transfer to a muslin/cheesecloth suspended over a suitable container. The liquid that leaches out

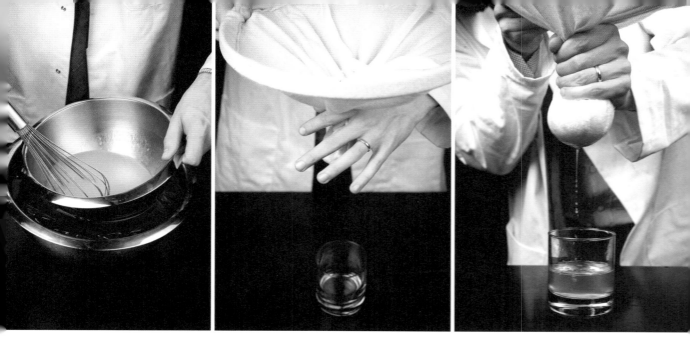

**ABOVE**: *Agar clarification*: 1. *Gently breaking a lime gel* 2. *Passing through a muslin* 3. *The (almost) clarified results*

should be almost totally clear. Some agitation of the muslin/cheesecloth may be required towards the end of the filtering, but don't get too aggressive, because cloudy agar particles can squeeze through.

Gelatine-freeze clarification can achieve similar results to agar clarification, but is considerably more time-consuming. This method requires you to make a refrigerated gelatine gel (5 g per 1 kg liquid) that then goes into the freezer (or can be frozen immediately with liquid nitrogen – see page 49). Once frozen solid, the jelly returns to the fridge to defrost, sat on a suitable muslin/cheesecloth filter. As the jelly defrosts, the structure fails and liquid leaches out, dripping through the cloth.

The only real benefit to this process is that the liquid doesn't need to be heated as much as with the agar method, but the effects of the heat are negligible and in my opinion the speed of the agar method vastly outweighs any slight negative effects of an additional 30°C/86°F heating.

## PECTIN ENZYME

Pectin is a gelling agent used a lot in the production of jams and sweets. It naturally occurs in plant cell walls and accounts for up to 2 per cent of the composition of fresh fruits and vegetables. Essentially it's part of the cement that holds a fruit together. For fruit and vegetable juices (which probably make up a large chunk of the products you intend on clarifying) this is a useful thing to know, as there are naturally occurring enzymes that break down pectin and therefore break down otherwise stable juices and purées. Pectinase, pectin lyase and pectinesterase are some enzymes that have been branded and commercially packaged and are available to buy online.

Whisk around 2 per cent pectin enzyme into cold apple juice and allow to sit for 12–24 hours. Clear liquid will float to the top and needs to be carefully poured off. Results are improved by sticking the liquid in a centrifuge (see pages 48–9). Pectin enzymes work best on fruits and vegetables with high pectin contents, especially apple and carrot juice. Low pH (high acidity) juices are a no-no.

## CHARCOAL FILTERING & CHILL FILTERING

Activated charcoal is carbon that has been treated with oxygen. It is unique and unrivalled in its surface-area-to-mass ratio. The more surface area, the better the chance that large impure molecules adsorb onto the surface of the charcoal. Charcoal filtering is best used as a finishing process to remove final traces of cloudiness and colour.

This type of filtration has been used to soften spirits for over two centuries. It's perhaps most famous for its use in the vodka-production process, mostly due to brands boasting about the number of times their spirit is filtered. But charcoal filtration features in the production of many spirits as a way of softening harsh characteristics and ensuring consistency. A common household water filter contains activated charcoal,

Many whiskies are chill-filtered. This process removes the haziness that can sometimes be caused by fatty acids and esters present within the aged liquid. As the name implies, the liquid is first chilled to around -1°C/30°F and then filtered through a cellulose or metal filter. The chilling results in some of the molecules clumping together to become a larger mass of particles, thus making them easier to remove.

## VACUUM FILTERING

Vacuum pumps and some vacuum packers can be put to good use by sucking liquid through fine filters. This can be used in conjunction with hydrocolloid filtration and simple filtering to speed up processes, or with finer-grade filters where gravity simply will not suffice.

The process normally involves some kind of specialist flask with a filter attached. The vacuum pump creates a low-pressure environment, drawing in liquids fine enough to squeeze through the filter. It's a much quicker process and much more effective than gravity alone.

## CENTRIFUGAL SEPARATION

At the top of the food chain and traditionally the most expensive option is the centrifuge. Centrifuges work by spinning liquids at incredibly high speeds (some spin at up to 70,000 RPM), exerting a gravitational pull on the liquid that is known commonly as g-force. This huge pull on the liquid causes the components to separate based on their density: oils float on top, solid particles sink and the bulk of the liquid phase sits somewhere in the middle. The same processes take place under the earth's normal gravitational pull, but at 30,000 g, a centrifuge amplifies the effect.

Add the centrifuge's abilities to some of the techniques listed above, such as enzymatic or jelly filtration, and you have a super-effective hybrid clarification process that will set you back a few pennies, but produce unrivalled results. A centrifuge can be used for all manner of applications, from separating the water out of tomato juice, to drawing a spirit back out of a pulpy infusion.

When I wrote my first book in 2013, a centrifuge would go for £5,000/$7,000 and only yield a couple of litres of useful product. They were not designed to be used in bars but in labs, and the price tag reflected that. The demand for these devices in cocktail bars has grown, though, and the availability of cheaper devices that will spin liquids quickly is evolving to meet that demand.

# DISTILLING

I'm fully aware that distilling one's own ingredients is not something that most home enthusiasts are likely to try, and in truth this is not something that goes on in most bars either. But distilling and redistilling products has been a staple part of my creative processes over the past eight years, as well as something I have become known for, so it would be negligent of me not to mention it.

Distilling, like fermentation, is part and parcel of many of the brands of liquor that feature in this book. Unlike fermentation, it requires at least some special equipment plus some caution where flammable alcohol vapours and potentially dangerous concentrations of toxic substances are concerned. Sounds like fun, right?

In some ways, distillation can be viewed as a process of infusion and clarification all tied up in one technique.

You boil the mixture of ingredients – water or alcohol, with fruits, herbs, flowers, or spices – then collect the vapour of that mixture and condense it back into a liquid. If the original liquid contained alcohol, there's a good chance the distilled liquid will have a higher concentration of alcohol in it because alcohol has a lower boiling point than water. The distilled product (or spirit) will also, hopefully, contain the concentrated aromatics of the other ingredients in your still too. 'Aromatics' is an important term here, since it is the 'aroma' of the ingredients – those elements that you can smell – that we are capturing here, not the taste.

Any type of still and condenser setup can be used to achieve this. On a commercial level, gin distillers use large pots to infuse the aromatic qualities of juniper and other botanicals into neutral spirit. These days it is much easier to source inexpensive 2–5-litre/quart copper pot stills that you can get great results from. Small distillation setups like this can be purchased for around £100/$140 or you can build your own using beakers, funnels and glass condensation units. I once built a small glass still from second-hand parts for under £50/$70, which used a pond pump to circulate ice water around the condensation unit. I'm fortunate enough to have made a bit of money since then, so in my bars we use a piece of equipment called a rotary evaporator (rotavap).

Distillation at normal atmospheric pressure requires quite a lot of heat, which can damage or denature certain ingredients like fruits, flowers and herbs. A rotavap is a lab-grade piece of distillation equipment that operates under a near vacuum and lowers the boiling point of everything inside it, eliminating heat-based spoilage and flavour damage derived from oxidation (since there is no oxygen).

Although it might look a little scary, a rotavap is basically made up of four sections: the water bath, which heats the mixture; the evaporating flask, which holds the mixture in the water bath and rotates (this is where the 'rotary' part of the name comes from), increasing the surface area of the mixture, promoting better evaporation; the condenser, which either takes the form of a liquid-nitrogen-filled 'cold finger' or a coiled tube filled with subzero coolant routed from a recirculating chiller; and a vacuum pump, which sucks all of the air out of the system.

Rotavaps were developed for labs, who loved them for their ability to slice away the components of a liquid based on their volatility. Once you get good at using a rotavap, and learn to balance air pressure with temperature, you can strip out extremely precise sections of an ingredient's aroma, like a painter selects colour from a palette.

I have used my rotavaps to make non-alcoholic spirits, for distilling peanut butter into bourbon whisky, and distilling pineapple husks into rum (see pages 146–7). I've also seen great results using a rotavap to concentrate fruit juices by distilling the water out (a concentrated juice that hasn't been heated tastes amazing) as well as for distilling aged Scotch and collecting the concentrated woody residue left behind to flavour cocktails with (as seen in my Insta-Age Rob Roy on page 153 in *The Curious Bartender*). There really is no end to the potential results you can achieve with a rotavap… it's just a shame that a full setup will set you back at least £5,000/$6,750.

It's worth noting that distilling alcohol in cocktail bars or even in your home in the UK and US is illegal unless you have the licence to do so. My development lab has a spirits compounder's licence, so our products are manufactured there.

# LIQUID NITROGEN

Liquid nitrogen (LN$_2$) is really useful stuff and far easier to get hold of these days than it used to be. You don't need a special licence to purchase it in the UK, but you do need to understand the risks involved with handling it and to never serve cocktails that contain liquid nitrogen. Nitrogen is a tool, not an ingredient.

Nitrogen gas in its liquid form is -196°C (-320.8°F), which is very cold indeed. A small splash of this stuff on your skin and you'll feed a prickle (or even tickle) of pain as it bounces off you and sublimates into the atmosphere. Larger splashes can cause cold burns, and nitrogen is particularly nasty when spilled onto loose clothing or shoes. Wear gloves if you like, but certainly invest in goggles and closed shoes.

Liquid nitrogen must be stored in a specialist dewar – a purpose-built pressurised vessel that is capable of maintaining a constant liquid state. However, even when stored in an expensive nitrogen dewar, the liquid will continue to evaporate through valves placed on the unit. Attempting to store liquid nitrogen in a sealed vessel will almost certainly result in an explosion.

Because it's always venting, your nitrogen dewar must be kept in a well-ventilated area. The nitrogen gas that is released from the dewar's valves is totally harmless, but when it bonds with oxygen atoms in the atmosphere, it forms nitrous oxide. This gas is not harmful either, but the reaction does deplete the surrounding air of the oxygen and so can cause asphyxiation. The problem is, you won't know you're being deprived of oxygen until you pass out. Store your nitrogen outside, or in a well-ventilated room, and never place yourself in an enclosed space with large amounts of liquid nitrogen.

Now on to the fun stuff – what can liquid nitrogen be used for? The first and most obvious use is freezing things. Liquid nitrogen will freeze pretty much anything, including spirits. Edible cocktail lollipops can be made with relative ease by submersing a lollipop mould into a bath of liquid nitrogen.

Liquid nitrogen can also be used as a bath for stirring cocktails in. Stirring down a Martini in liquid nitrogen means that the drink can be served as low as –30°C/-22°F, which is a lower temperature than a domestic freezer can get to. You can also use liquid nitrogen to quickly chill glasses by pouring a splash into the glass and quickly swirling.

Liquid nitrogen can also be used to make ice cream. Production of alcoholic ice cream is a laborious process to perform with a conventional freezer or with an ice-cream maker, but with liquid nitrogen it's achievable in under a minute. Besides time, the other advantage to making $LN_2$ ice cream is that the speed of freezing forms smaller ice crystals, so the texture feels creamier.

Finally, you can also use liquid nitrogen to quickly infuse spirits with fruit or herbs. Douse the ingredient in nitrogen and, once it's frozen solid, smash it up with a muddler or anything heavy. Once the ingredient is powdered, pour spirit over and marvel as the flavour and colour quickly infuses (see pages 37–9).

# SMOKING

The first person to ever serve me a smoked cocktail was my chef friend, Tristan Welch. I was conducting a series of rum-themed training sessions across the UK and Tristan was co-hosting with me, tasked with making cocktails using culinary techniques. In our first session together he produced a handheld smoking device, fittingly called a 'smoking gun', and proceeded to pump applewood smoke onto the surface of a drink, then place a little glass lid on it. Over time the smoke slipped into the fabric of the rum and when the lid was released the effect was a fantastic smoke-infused liquid.

I was mightily impressed that it could be so easy to add a desirable smoky flavour to a drink in a matter of seconds. When my first bar, Purl, opened I was very keen to have a smoked drink on our first menu, in part because nobody else was doing it. The result was a Rum Old Fashioned cocktail called 'Mr Hyde's Fixer Upper', which featured a smoke-injected, wax-sealed potion bottle accompanied by a tea-scented dry-ice fog. The drink was incredibly theatrical for its time and one of the main reasons why Purl was such a hit. Guests would walk into the bar and simply ask for the 'smoky drink' without a glance at the menu.

Nine years have passed since then and my understanding of smoke and smoked drinks has come a long way. Since the release of *The Curious Bartender: The*

*Artistry and Alchemy of Creating the Perfect Cocktail* (when smoked drinks were still quite uncommon) I have seen and tasted smoked cocktails all over the world. Some of these drinks have been delicious, but I'm sorry to say that many have not.

The problem with many of these drinks is the conflict between a balanced flavour of smoke and the visual impact of smoke. You cannot have it both ways. If smoke is visibly in contact with your drink, it is changing its flavour, and since you wouldn't be comfortable with a cocktail that periodically dispenses more lime juice into your drink, you shouldn't be comfortable with a drink like this either. Even mixing drinks with smoke is, at best, an art that few people have mastered, and at its worst, impossible to do with any level of consistency. You can't measure smoke any more than you can grab hold of it. It's for these reasons that I choose to smoke my cocktails before mixing them, usually by smoking an individual ingredient and then adjusting its smokiness by diluting back with the same (unsmoked) ingredient. This allows for a good degree of fine tuning and consistent, repeatable results.

To get the best possible smoke flavour, it's useful to understand some of the science that's at play. Smoke is produced by burning wood. Below 300°C/570°F most of the smoke produced by smouldering wood is a result of cellulose and hemicellulose breaking down. This kind of smoke can smell a bit nasty, as it contains some of the more acrid and astringent compounds produced by burning wood. Most of the positive aromatic effects of smoke derive from the breaking down of the lignin present within the wood. Lignin is a compound that makes up around a quarter of the structure of wood (but varies according to the type of wood) and when it reaches temperatures of over 300°C/570°F it breaks down into complex aromatic molecules called carbonyls and phenols. It's these compounds that contribute the typical sweet and spicy aromatics to food such as vanilla, maple, caramel, nut, clove and cherry. As the temperature of the wood increases to 400°C/750°F, the smoke becomes denser, almost liquid-like, and it's at this stage that it carries the best flavours and the bulk of the aromatic compounds.

Creep too high, though, and there's a risk that the wood will catch fire (smoking drinks is proof that there can be smoke without fire!). At this stage the wood temperature increases to 1,000°C/1,830°F – which is bad for those precious aromatics.

The cheapest and easiest way to impart smoke into a drink is to use a handheld smoking device. These come in many shapes and forms, from budget models (under £20/$28) up to more elaborate versions (over £200/$285). Of course, you get what you pay for, and I'm personally a big fan of the Polyscience smoking gun, which costs around £60/$85. It's durable, reasonably easy to clean and very effective.

The gun section has a steel crucible with a standard pipe filter. The wood is placed in the crucible then ignited with a flame. A switch turns a fan on that draws the smoke into the device and then out through a flexible pipe. The smoke can be easily directed into a vessel, cloche, mixing beaker or glass. The draw of air through the crucible causes the smouldering wood to heat sufficiently without catching alight. If the temperature of the wood reaches 500°C/930°F there is a danger that the wood will spontaneously combust, but this can be controlled by restricting airflow into the crucible. Here's how the process goes: place the wood in the crucible and switch on the motor. Ignite the wood with a flame or chef's blowtorch (blow out the flame if necessary). Allow the smoke to build in colour and density for 5 seconds. Then direct the flow of smoke.

Clean your smoker regularly, as aromatic oils released by the burning of wood can build up inside the device.

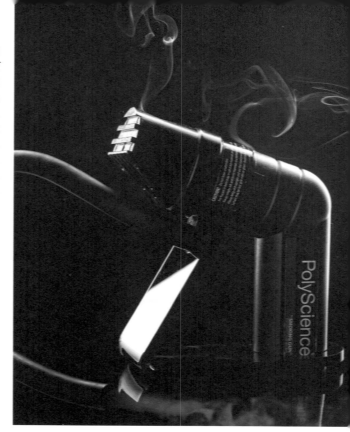

The repeated heating and cooling of these oils can result in them being broken down into foul-smelling compounds that will degrade smoke quality significantly.

The type of wood you use will have a bearing on the type of smoke that is produced. Much of the aromatic intensity of wood is a result of the lignin content; lower-lignin woods produce less aromatic, more acrid smokes, while higher-lignin woods (such as mesquite) produce more aromatically intense smokes. Below are my favourite smoking woods.

HICKORY

*Sweet aromatic aroma, typically used in barbecues*

APPLE

*Lighter aromatic, but a pleasant fruity characteristic*

OAK

*Very bold and intense; use carefully so as not to overpower*

MESQUITE

*Strong and rich aromatics*

# MATURING

Aged cocktails are nothing new. After all, we've been storing wine and beer in barrels for millennia, so why not mixed drinks too? The world's first mixologists stored their drinks in bottles for later use, and bottled cocktails even became marketable products at the turn of the 20th century (as they are again today). The Heublein company advertised their 'wood-aged' cocktails in America as far back as 1906, and continued to do so right through to the 1930s. One advert from *Theatre Magazine* in July 1906, read:

'A delicious cocktail that's always ready for you or your guest – and better than any made by guesswork effort can be. CLUB COCKTAILS are scientifically blended of fine old liquors and aged in wood to exquisite aroma and smoothness.'

By the time you read this, the pre-eminent mixologists of today (in an effort to recreate anything and everything that was built, shaken or stirred during the early 20th century) have probably aged pretty much every cocktail you can think of – with predictably mixed results. The truth of the matter is that where barrels are concerned, there's often far too little concern for what the drink actually tastes like (and far too much emphasis on the 'story' behind it). The problem is that, in reference to barrels and cocktails, there's very little literature to reference. Instead, we must revert to reading spirits-production manuals along with good old trial and error (the trick to trial and error is knowing when you are in error!).

My top tip for all kinds of ageing is this: don't be afraid to correct your cocktail after you've matured it. There is an extremely high likelihood that the cocktail you pull out of a barrel or bottle is not the best possible version of that drink. So do as you would do in any other situation: taste it, adjust it, perfect it.

## BARREL AGEING

Barrel ageing is definitely the most complex of the ageing techniques that I use, because the wood itself is an ingredient, and an unpredictable one at that.

Barrels come in all sorts of sizes, varieties and conditions. The type of cask you use (which will probably be under 50 litres/53 quarts in capacity) will hugely affect the final flavour of your drink. New oak casks will work quickly to impart flavour, whereas casks that are on their second or third fills will naturally have a decreased effect. You can acquire casks that have previously held other liquids – sherry, wine and bourbon, to name a few – as well as choose between differing char and toasting levels. The size of the cask affects the surface-area-to-liquid ratio, with smaller casks imparting some flavours much faster than larger ones. It's important to recognise that all of these factors, as well as time, will have distinct consequences on the drink that comes out of the barrel.

Oak itself contains over 100 volatile components capable of contributing flavour to a cocktail. Additionally there are other compounds formed through the oxidation of wood extracts and compounds already present in the drink (which may itself contain aged ingredients!). Chromatography reveals that a number of phenolic compounds and furanic aldehydes are produced as a result of barrel-ageing. These compounds define what we recognise as the key flavour identifiers of aged products - dry, vanilla, nutty, resinous, fruity, sweet and toasted characteristics, to name a few. We can break down the reactions that produce these flavours into three categories: infusion, oxidation and extraction.

When storing your barrel between uses, always keep a small amount of water in there and leave the bung off the top. This will keep the barrel from drying out and prevent bacteria from growing in the barrel.

## INFUSION

Infusion refers to all the 'good stuff' that a spirit or cocktail will take directly from the wood. Think of a cask as a reverse teabag, a highly compacted cylinder of flavour. The charring or toasting process that occurs on the inside surface of the cask breaks down the various structures of the wood into shorter chained sugars that infuse directly into the liquid. The additive effects of the wood come from four potential sources that make up much of the composition of oak – lignin, hemicellulose, extractives and oak tannins.

Most of the 'wood' flavour that we are familiar with, like vanilla, butter, caramel, banana and coconut, are formed as a result of the breakdown of lignin – a part of the secondary cell wall of the wood. Vanillin, responsible for the vanilla flavour, naturally occurs – surprise surprise – most abundantly in vanilla (around 2 per cent composition by weight) and is responsible for vanilla's claim to being the second most popular flavour in the world (chocolate is first, but it also contains vanillin, as does breast milk). Of course vanilla and vanillin are not always welcome guests and do have a tendency to take over the party, but with a clear presence in aged spirits there is certainly a relevance and a basis for a little vanillin manipulation in aged cocktails. The breakdown of lignin at higher levels can also provide toasty, smoky flavours too.

All barrel-aged drinks will extract a certain amount of tannin from the wood. Tannin is more prevalent in European casks as opposed to American, and contributes a great deal towards the colour of an aged spirit. On the palate it is apparent as a strange drying sensation, and if carefully integrated, can add welcome structure and balance to a drink.

## OXIDATION

Oxidation is a crucial part of ageing some spirits and wines. It aids in the development and complexity of the liquid. The oxidation of ethanol (alcohol) converts to acetaldehyde, the compound responsible for sherry-like nutty, grassy notes. It is this oxidative effect that provides sherry and vermouth (vermouth also being partially oxidised during production) with their characteristic finish.

The subject of sherry actually has a great relevance to the barrel-ageing debate. Oloroso sherry is a marriage of wine and spirit that is aged in cask – in fact, the same ingredients (in principle) that are used to make a Martinez or a Manhattan – spirit, wine and bitters. On that basis, I think it's hard to dismiss the very concept of barrel-ageing cocktails, as some do, when the same theory applies to such great effect in the production of sherries.

Continuing with acetaldehyde, it can in turn be oxidised itself, converting into acetic acid. Acetic acid in small quantities provides a 'bite' and 'fullness' to a cocktail, but in larger levels can add a harsh edge and so must be closely monitored. Wine oxidises and spoils much more quickly than spirits, so most common barrel-aged cocktails have a kind of safety barrier, thanks to being higher in ABV and sporting a greater resilience to the effects of oxygen.

## EXTRACTION

Extraction is all about the softening of the drink. This process is thought to occur thanks to the presence of hemicellulose within the wood (around 15–25 per cent of the total composition of oak). Hemicellulose reacts with acids present within the liquid and produces complex reducing sugars. It is believed to be these sugars that slightly soften the drink, as well as giving the effect of integration and consistency. Interestingly, it's thought that a higher acidity will result in a greater softening effect, which is exactly why drinks containing vermouth work so well. For the particularly inspired amongst you, experimenting with bolstering the acid content of your cocktails before ageing may yield interesting results.

These are just some of the effects of barrel-ageing cocktails. Clearly, there are many factors to consider and it is not simply a case of putting a drink in wood and hoping for the best. However, careful consideration of the forces at work can and does yield fantastic results.

## BOTTLE AGEING

It might sound silly to suggest that putting a drink in a glass bottle, sealing it, then waiting for a while, is likely to achieve anything other than a greater level of thirst. It's generally accepted that spirits do not age in bottles – the ABV is simply too high – but research now suggests that may not be entirely true. Over the course of years vintage wines will mature, mellow and develop complexity in the bottle. Since strong cocktails are generally about halfway between the ABV of wine and spirits (25–32 per cent typically, once diluted), perhaps it isn't crazy to suggest some development may occur?

I have personally conducted triangular taste tests on aged cocktails versus fresh ones and there are indeed distinguishable differences – a harmony of flavours, softening of alcohol – but it's hard to put a finger on exactly what it is. There are a bunch of theories that attempt to explain what happens when a cocktail or spirit is left in a bottle for a period of time, but much of it at the time of writing is still conjecture.

One of my favourite explanations, which came from Scott Spolverino, is that alcohol molecules and water molecules do not mix evenly at 20 per cent ABV and above and that ethanol molecules tend to cluster over time. It's possible that a newly mixed cocktail containing unaged spirits is more heterogeneously mixed and therefore harsher on the palate. As the cocktail rests, the alcohol molecules tightly cluster together, meaning that the drink slips down all the better!

# CARBONATION

A little bit of fizz can be a great thing in a cocktail, and although it's true that not all drinks feel a benefit from being bubbly, it's also a fact that some drinks do not work without them.

A fizzy mixer (soda water, tonic, cola) is the easiest way to get some sparkle into your cocktails, but there are downsides to them, such as the limited range of flavours and the dilution of fizz from other, non-carbonated ingredients. If you can afford the time and effort, you'll find that carbonating your own drinks can be a very rewarding strategy in the pursuit of perfection. And in doing so, you will bring about a ton of new options in respect to the types of drinks that can be made to fizz and pop, as well as the chance to fine-tune the fizz level of your creations.

## HOW BUBBLES WORK

That prickly sting of bubbles in the mouth is caused by $CO_2$ bubbles triggering our tongue's sour receptors. The effect is not fully understood by scientists, but can be broadly classed as a highly localised sensation of acidity that can become painful if the drink has been heavily carbonated. The important thing to note here is that it's the $CO_2$ itself rather than the physical bursting of the bubble that produces that feeling of fizz. Were the bubbles to be made from another gas, like air, oxygen or nitrogen (as is the case with some foams and whipped cream), the same stinging sensation could not be felt.

The fizziness of a liquid depends on two factors: the pressure of the $CO_2$ in the liquid, and the temperature of the liquid.

If you pump loads of $CO_2$ inside a bottle you increase the pressure in the bottle. This forces some of the $CO_2$ to dissolve into your cocktail, which makes your drink more fizzy. If your bottle has lots of headspace you need to put proportionally more $CO_2$ in there per millilitre/fluid ounce of liquid to increase the headspace pressure and produce a fizzy liquid.

A cold liquid can hold more $CO_2$ than a warmer one. You can prove this to yourself by squeezing the headspace of a warm plastic bottle of unopened soda and a cold bottle of unopened soda. The warm bottle will feel firmer because less of the $CO_2$ is in solution

and more of it is pressurising the headspace. In practice, the relationship between temperature and fizziness means that you should always carbonate liquids when they are cold, and warm drinks lose their fizz faster.

Losing fizz isn't always a bad thing. For a cocktail to look fizzy in a glass we ask that the $CO_2$ forms bubbles that rise to the surface. Equally, when we take a sip on a cold glass of Champagne, the warm environment of your mouth causes bubbles to form out of the solution and prickle our mouths. The colder your mouth is, the less fizzy your drink feels because fewer bubbles emerge from the solution.

Once in the glass, your drink will lose fizz quickly because the relatively low atmospheric pressure of planet earth is insufficient to keep all that $CO_2$ dissolved. The surface of the glass offers one escape route for the gas, which is why narrower glasses (like Champagne flutes) hold fizz longer. The second way that gas leaves is by bubbles that form on the inside of the glass. A bubble is born on the small imperfections in the glass known as nucleation points, which is another way of saying 'rough bits'. Without nucleation points you won't get any bubbles at all – a perfectly smooth glass (you'll do well to find one) will form no bubbles, no matter how fizzy the drink is. Some glasses are purposely scratched on the inside of their bases to promote the nucleation of bubbles. But any imperfection will do, from floating bits of organic matter to cloth fibres and lumps of sugar.

## MEASURING CARBONATION

The amount of $CO_2$ in your drink can be expressed as grams per litre (g/l). A 330-ml/11-fl. oz. can of Coke has around 2.1 g of $CO_2$ in it, which equates to around 6.3 grams per litre. Fruit sodas tend to have a little less, at about 5 g/l and some effervescent waters have less than 3 g/l which explains why the fizz can sometimes feel a little lacklustre. For non-alcoholic drinks, anything above 8 g/l of $CO_2$ begins to get painful. But g/l of $CO_2$ in a non-alcoholic liquid only tells us half the story.

$CO_2$ is more soluble in alcohol than it is in water. This might lead you to assume that a boozy drink with 5 g/l of $CO_2$ will taste more fizzy than a non-alcoholic drink with the same amount of $CO_2$ in it.

In fact, the reverse is true. Because $CO_2$ is so at home in alcohol, it is less inclined to leave and form bubbles. This is why alcoholic drinks need a higher pressure of carbonation than non-alcoholic ones to produce the same perception of fizziness. Some Champagnes (which sit at about 12 per cent ABV) contain as much as 12 g/l of $CO_2$, which, if successfully dissolved into water, would be undrinkable.

In practice, measuring carbonation is rather tricky to do, but standard carbonation levels can be useful as references, especially if you're planning on trying my dry ice carbonation method (see page 59). Ultimately, the best way to get the right level of fizz in your drinks is to taste them and adjust your methods accordingly.

## RULES FOR CARBONATION KINGS & QUEENS

However you choose to carbonate your drinks, you will need to follow some simple rules to get the best results.

The first rule is to always use cold liquids – the colder the better. Since you're likely to be serving a cold cocktail in the first instance, this shouldn't prove too much of a challenge. Chill your drink in the fridge (or better yet, give it a blast in the freezer) prior to carbonating. You won't want it to be slushy, mind, as this gives the gas a whole load of nucleation points and your drink will fizz all over the place.

Next you will want to ensure your drink is clear. In fact, you'll probably want to do that before chilling, since some filtering may be required. Insoluble particles in your cocktail will cause the drink to froth when you carbonate it, so use the appropriate filtering (see page 45) and clarification (see pages 46–8) methods before you start. Note that your drinks don't need to be colourless, they just need to be transparent (not opaque).

All carbonation methods require you to repeat the carbonation process at least once. This is to remove air that naturally places itself in the container you're carbonating into, and it needs flushing out. You can't carbonate with air, and more air in your container means less $CO_2$, which means less fizz. You'll never remove all of the air from your bottle/siphon but repeated carbonation and venting will dramatically improve efficiency and reward you with next-level fizz in your drinks.

When carbonating you will also want to agitate the liquid as much as possible. This might seem counter-intuitive, since shaking a bottle of soda is such an effective – not to mention, fun – way of removing $CO_2$ from the liquid. Soda foams when shaken because its surface area is greatly increased, even though the container stays the same size. The gas exits the liquid rapidly and charges up the neck of the bottle, carrying liquid with it as foam. Shaking during carbonation is effective for the same reasons, but in this instance we're increasing the surface area to help push $CO_2$ into the liquid rather than take it out. Agitation needn't always be a case of shaking, though – a SodaStream (see page 58) uses jets of very small bubbles to increase the surface contact area of $CO_2$ and liquid.

Finally, it's best to avoid drinks that contain protein (egg white, whey, aquafaba) or any kind of surfactant that is likely to create a foam, such as lecithin.

## MAKING A CARBONATION RIG

Although it may look and sound terrifying, it's actually really simple to build a carbonation rig using a $CO_2$ tank, regulator and hose. The initial outlay of equipment shouldn't set you back more than £100/$140 and you'll be able to carbonate hundreds of litres of liquid with it at a low ongoing cost.

A carbonation rig is great for a bar where you're likely to be carbonating a lot of liquid, but you may prefer a smaller, less industrial-looking solution like a SodaStream if you're making drinks at home. $CO_2$ tanks can be picked up from welding-supply shops and websites, or from cellar-supply companies. I prefer 5-litre tanks as they are compact enough to fit anywhere but big enough to last a while. You may need to leave a deposit for the tank itself, then just pay for and switch it with a full tank when you run out. Always keep your tank chained to a wall to stop it from falling over – these things rarely rupture, but it can do some damage to your feet if you knock it over by accident.

The enormous pressure held inside a $CO_2$ tank (60 bar, or over six times the pressure produced by an espresso machine) needs dropping down to sensible levels for drinks carbonation. The kind of regulator you need will drop the pressure down to between 0 and 4 bar, which is perfect for bar work, since most drinks need around 2.5–3 bar of pressure. Expect to pay no more than £30/$42 for a regulator.

Next you'll need plastic soda bottles, a ball-lock gas fitting and carbonator cap, and some reinforced hose to connect it to the regulator. These bits can be purchased from home-brew websites at little cost. The cap goes on your bottle and the ball-lock fitting goes in the cap, creating a tight seal into which to pump the gas.

## USING A CARBONATION RIG

Set your regulator to the correct pressure (2.5–3 bar) and turn on the gas – don't worry, it won't come out until you connect the ball-lock onto the bottle. Fill your plastic bottle three-quarters full with chilled liquid then squeeze as much of the remaining air out of the bottle as possible. Next, screw on the carbonator cap to the top of your bottle. If you're carbonating lots of bottles I suggest getting more carbonator caps and filling/squeezing all of them, as this will speed up the next part.

Clip the ball-lock connector onto the carbonator cap and marvel at how the bottle inflates and the headspace pressurises. Give it a good shake. No, harder than that! After shaking, disconnect the ball-lock fixing and unscrew the carbonator cap a touch. The drink will foam slightly. Once it's done its thing, screw the cap back on, connect the ball-lock fixing and shake again. Finally, disconnect the ball-lock and let the bottle rest in the fridge. If you have more bottles to carbonate, just repeat the above steps.

If you want to store your drinks in glass, you can carefully decant them out of plastic after carbonation and use a bottle capper to seal them. I wouldn't recommend carbonating directly into glass bottles for two reasons. Firstly, you can't squeeze the air out of glass, which makes it much harder to get $CO_2$ into the drink. Secondly, there's no pressure feedback mechanism as there is with the flexibility of a plastic bottle. Some glass bottles can have manufacturing defects that weaken them and you really don't want the surprise of an exploding glass bottle.

## SODASTREAM

The friendliest form of carbonation in the home and a highly usable – if a little more expensive – means of carbonation in a bar.

As the child of the 1980s, the SodaStream was a mechanical miracle of the kitchen. My feelings towards it today haven't changed much. The SodaStream is compact, easy to use, and relatively inexpensive. They are great bits of kit for carbonating water at home (and SodaStream would rather you kept it to only water), but can also be used for carbonating mixed drinks, as long as you keep to the rules.

As with other forms of carbonation, it's essential that you use cold liquids to begin with, as this greatly improves the liquid's ability to dissolve $CO_2$ and makes for a fizzier cocktail. Also, like other carbonation techniques, you need to purge the flask/vessel of air

so that it's purely $CO_2$ that you're forcing into the drink. This means repeating the process twice or three times, which means you'll get through SodaStream's proprietary gas canisters rather quickly, too.

The main trick with SodaStream is to not attempt to carbonate too much at a time. This is due to the tendency for the drink to foam, and you really want to avoid that foam getting gunked up in the pressure-release valve at the top of the machine. Golden rule: never fill the bottle more than half full (one-third is about right) and vent the bottle very carefully between blasts of $CO_2$.

## SODA SYPHON/ISI WHIPPER/ TWIST'N SPARKLE

Cream whippers and syphons are the carbonation bar tools that most bartenders naturally turn to first. After all, syphons have been around for nearly 200 years and their design is iconic as a cocktail shaker or Martini glass. An iSi whipper is intended to be used for making foams using nitrogen gas, but it happily takes $CO_2$ canisters and does the same job as a syphon. A Twist'n Sparkle is a newer innovation from iSi that takes on the form of a bottle and has no valve to eject the contents out of.

All three pieces of kit do exactly the same thing, the only difference being the way in which the manufacturer intends you to dispense the liquid once you've carbonated it. If you were going to buy only one of them, make sure you go for the iSi whipper. It can do everything the other two can do, as well as make foams.

The first syphon was invented in 1829, when two Frenchmen patented a kind of hollow corkscrew, which could be inserted into a soda bottle and, by use of a valve, allowed a portion of the fizzy water to be dispensed while maintaining the pressure on the inside of the bottle and preventing the remaining soda from going flat.

Modern syphons came about in the late 19th century and today they use 7.5-g $CO_2$ cartridges. The process involves injecting the gas into the syphon headspace by screwing the cartridge onto a one-way valve. The gas performs two roles here: carbonating the contents as well as creating positive pressure inside the system that forces the liquid back out again when you press a lever valve. The valve is connected to a tube that draws from the bottom of the syphon so you can dispense fizz while the syphon is standing upright; iSi (cream) whippers work exactly the same way, except the device expects you to be dispensing foams (made with $N_2O$) so you don't get the tube. This means that when using an iSi whipper it is better to carbonate your drink then simply unscrew the cap and pour the contents out (you can do this with a syphon too, but you lose a bit of the theatre). The Twist'n Sparkle has no lever valve, so you have to unscrew the top to get to the liquid.

While syphons and whippers are easy to use and look great, there are a few downsides that put them lower on my list of preferred carbonation methods.

For one, they are expensive. A single unit will tend to set you back about £40/$55, which isn't so bad, but the cartridges themselves cost around £1/$1.40 each, and since you'll need at least two every time you want to carbonate something, the costs of producing a drink like this can quickly mount up.

The valve mechanisms on these things are ideal breeding grounds for mould, especially if you leave the lid screwed on with no airflow for an extended period. You'll also find that the valves stick unless everything is super-clean and sterile. You'll know if the valve has stuck because when you charge the device the gas will pour straight back out of the nozzle. Sticky valves are a good way of wasting those expensive $CO_2$ canisters.

The same principles apply here as with other carbonation methods. Always use cold liquids, and take time to chill down your syphon/whipper too. Give the unit a really good shake when carbonating, then vent the gas and repeat. If you're using a syphon you will need to turn it upside down when you vent, otherwise you'll spray your drink everywhere. You will need to carbonate a second, and possibly third time if you're looking for good bubbles.

# DRY ICE

Dry ice is carbon dioxide in its solid state and its temperature is around -79°C/-110°F. It's a great tool for its sublimation properties (it evaporates straight from a solid to a gas, thus skipping the liquid phase) and can be used to make aromatic 'fogs' by pouring warm infusions over it. Dry ice does burn skin on contact though, so it should always be handled with gloves and the appropriate utensils.

It's possible to use dry ice to carbonate drinks, but I'll preface this... I wouldn't unless I had none of the other techniques available to me. If you're not careful, it can have explosive results! That said, it's a quick, cost-effective way of fizzing drinks, and quite rock 'n' roll.

The premise is simple. Decide how fizzy you want your cocktail and calculate an appropriate weight of $CO_2$ to carbonate it with. Remember how I mentioned that a litre of Coke has around 6.3 g of $CO_2$ in it? Well, there's a good place to start.

As usual, you will need to use very cold liquid and a plastic (PET) bottle with a screw-on cap. Half fill your bottle with cocktail and calculate the weight of $CO_2$ you will need based on the volume of liquid (not the volume of the bottle). Weigh out the correct amount of dry ice (the small 9 mm pellets you get tend to weigh about 2 g) to the weight you require, being careful not to burn yourself. Drop the pellet in the bottle and loosely screw on the cap. Leave the pellet to sublimate for 30 seconds. Since $CO_2$ weighs more than air, this will slowly push the air out through the top of the bottle. Now seal the bottle tight and shake like your life depends on it.

All being well, the dry ice will fully sublimate and you will have yourself a pressurised bottle of fizz. Allow it to sit for a couple of minutes before opening (carefully).

PART III

# THE COCKTAILS

# LIGHT

CHAMPAGNE COCKTAIL

CORPSE REVIVER
NO. 2

TOM COLLINS

AMERICANO

BULLSHOT

WHITE LADY

SHERRY COBBLER

# DRY

VODKA MARTINI

BREAKFAST MARTINI

PISCO SOUR

LAST WORD

HANKY-PANKY

JACK ROSE

## THE FLAVOUR MAP
Use this 'flavour map' to decide
which classic cocktail fits your
needs. Each drink's position on
the page is based on how light,
rich, dry or sweet it is.

# RICH

# LIGHT

BRONX

GUNFIRE

LONG ISLAND
ICED TEA

TEQUILA SUNRISE

BATANGA

BLUE LAGOON

WHITE RUSSIAN

EL DIABLO

# SWEET

RUM SWIZZLE

SANGRIA

CORN 'N' OIL

WHISKY MAC

HARVARD

BOBBY BURNS

VIEUX CARRÉ

RUSTY NAIL

BOULEVARDIER

# RICH

BLUE BLAZER

# BRANDY

# HARVARD

50 ML/1⅔ FL. OZ. HENNESSY FINE DE COGNAC
20 ML/⅔ FL. OZ. MARTINI ROSSO
10 ML/⅓ FL. OZ. WATER
2 DASHES ANGOSTURA BITTERS

Add all of the ingredients to a mixing beaker and stir for 30–40 seconds.
Strain into a chilled coupe glass. Garnish with orange zest.

The Harvard is unquestionably the lesser known of the dark spirit, vermouth and bitters family of cocktails (it's the Manhattan and Rob Roy that sit at the head ends of that particular table). But – and I fully appreciate that this is a bold statement – it might just be shining star of the household.

In spite of the capability of Cognac and brandy as cocktail ingredients, their impending renaissance period appears to be on permanent hold. Great liquid credentials is one thing, but the ongoing identity crisis of Cognac, which is made and governed mostly by old men in large châteaux, and bought and consumed by young men in nightclubs, places the category in a particularly weird sort of paradox where the people Cognac is marketed at are not the people who are drinking it. For the bar enthusiast, however, there's nothing to stop us from appreciating this great liquid and mixing with it

regularly. It is, after all, one of the original mixing spirits of mid-19th-century America.

The Harvard first found its name in ink in George J. Kappeler's 1895 book, *Modern American Drinks*. Kappeler's recipe called for sugar, Angostura bitters (three dashes), equal parts Italian vermouth and brandy, as well as seltzer water. That's a high proportion of vermouth to brandy, which would result in a slightly flabby cocktail, so perhaps the intention was to soften up that boisterous combination? Naturally I have tried the drink this way and I for one found the slight fizz to be a bit too much of a distraction from the elegant union of grape spirit and grape wine in a glass. Granted, the drink benefits from a little extra dilution, and it's not a cocktail that needs to be served ice cold either, so I wouldn't grumble if a bartender added half a measure of water to the mixing beaker before stirring.

# FOX CLUB

· · · · · · · · · · · · · · · · · · · · · · · · · · · · · · · · · · · · · · · · · · · · · · · · · ·

450 ML/15¼ FL. OZ. HENNESSY XO COGNAC • 150 ML/5 FL. OZ. CARPANO ANTICA FORMULA
100 ML/3½ FL. OZ. PERIQUE TOBACCO LIQUEUR • 5 ML/1 TEASPOON ABBOT'S BITTERS
100 ML/3½ FL. OZ. WATER
*Suitable for a 1-litre/quart bota – makes 10 cocktails*

Rinse your *bota* with cold water. Mix the ingredients together and fill the skin using a funnel. Screw on the cap and allow the liquid to rest. Don't allow your cocktail to mature for too long, as the leather and resin flavour will become overpowering. In the event that the leather flavour does become too strong, remove the liquid from the bota and dilute it using more unaged cocktail until you find the right balance. To make the drink, stir 80 ml/2¾ fl. oz. of aged cocktail over cubed ice for 1 minute, then strain into a chilled cocktail glass.

The Fox Club is one of Harvard University's six all-male final clubs, which collectively serve as the last bastions of male exclusivity and aristocracy left at the school. Whether you're a member or not (and let's face it – you're not), their presence profoundly shapes the social and political culture on campus. I figure I'll probably never kick back with a Cohiba cigar in the ventilated smoking room of 44 John F. Kennedy Street, but by christening this drink Fox Club at least now there's a chance that one of my cocktails will be served there.

But what does a Fox Club cocktail taste like? Well, it would need to be based on the Harvard cocktail (obviously) and should be representative of the activities that go on in the club as well as the look, feel and smell of the clubhouse. Which, to broadly summarise (based on no actual experience of the clubhouse and having never met a single one of the club's members) is: drinking and smoking in leather armchairs.

Leather and tobacco then. Shouldn't be too hard.

Animal skins and organs have been used by us lot to store liquids for thousands of years. They proved to be good at holding fluids because, well, that is precisely their intended purpose in nature. In the production of the traditional Spanish *bota* (or wineskin) bag, the receptacle is made from goat leather then either lined with the goat's bladder or painted on the inside with a juniper or pine-based resin to prevent leakages. Shepherds in the Basque region call these bottles *zahato* and drink from them *zurrust*, meaning to spray a jet of water or wine in

to your mouth without the nozzle of the skin touching your lips.

There are still a handful of Spanish wineskin producers that follow the old techniques: drying and tanning goatskin using the shredded bark of pine, oak and mimosa trees, stitching the skin into a pouch, then sealing the inside with juniper resin. Since these products are intended for holding stuff you're going to drink, it also makes them suitable for storing cocktails and, indeed, flavouring them with leather.

The rules that apply here are similar to barrel ageing. With water or wine you're likely to extract a small amount of leather and juniper flavour from the skin, particularly on the first few fills. In the case of a cocktail, with a much higher alcohol content, the extraction of flavour is more extreme, and can continue over many repeat fillings. By deliberately imbuing the flavour of the skin in the cocktail, it's possible to impart a subtle leather fragrance to the drink. Extra emphasis on the 'subtle' though, as the strong taste of leather will be akin to licking a sofa, which isn't fun. Fortunately, where cocktails are concerned, we have the luxury of being able to blend unaged ingredients into aged ones, thus balancing the effects of the container.

I'm modifying this classic Harvard with a touch of Perique liqueur, made by Ted Breaux, a chemist turned spirits producer. It's the only commercially produced liqueur made from tobacco that avoids all the dangerous components of tobacco but still captures the good stuff.

· · · · · · · · · · · · · · · · · · · · · · · · · · · · · · · · · · · · · · · · · · · · · · · · · ·

# JACK ROSE

60 ML/2 FL. OZ. LAIRD'S APPLEJACK • 15 ML/½ FL. OZ. LEMON JUICE
7.5 ML/1½ TEASPOONS GRENADINE

Shake all the ingredients with cubed ice and strain into a chilled Martini glass.

The base of this drink is applejack, otherwise known as colonial America's answer to Calvados. It's a drink made from the 'jacking' (as in 'jack-up' or 'increase') of hard cider into potent spirit. 'Jacking' is not the same as distilling, though. Instead of being heated, the boozy apple juice is frozen and then defrosted but only the first liquids that defrost (which are higher in alcoholic strength) are collected. The process is repeated a few times to get the strength up and above 40 per cent ABV. It's as basic as they come (and not as efficient a process as using a heated still), which means a lower-strength spirit that has some associated risks, as no account is taken for the dangerous higher alcohols and ketones that are usually stripped out in pot distillation. The result, though, is some rather punchy juice, full of raw, agricultural, apple flavours, which leaves behind the gift of a headache to remember it by.

Given how primitive the production of applejack is, you'd be right to think it has a long history in North America. By the late 19th century, applejack was quickly falling out of favour in the US, supplanted by good imported brandy, home-grown whiskey, and other spirits of higher repute made using better technological standards (basically any other spirit). That's why it's surprising that the Jack Rose cocktail – applejack's only major player in the mixed drinks arena – was invented.

The drink was first mentioned in *The National Police Gazette* on 22 April 1905, under a job advertisement titled 'An Athletic Mixologist'. The ad was posted by 'Frank J. May, better known as Jack Rose, [who] is the inventor of a very popular cocktail by that name'.

May was, at the time, running Gene Sullivan's Café at 187 Pavonia Avenue in New Jersey. As for the mention of 'athletic' in the title, the advert informs us

that, 'May takes an active interest in sports, and as a wrestler could give many of the professional wrestlers a warm argument.'

Shortly after, in 1908, the Jack Rose makes its first appearance in a cocktail book: *Jack's Manual on the Vintage and Production, Care and Handling of Wines and Liquors* by J. A. Grohusko. The recipe calls for '10 dashes raspberry syrup, 10 dashes lemon juice, 5 dashes orange juice, juice of half a lime, and 75% cider brandy'. Then we're instructed to: 'Fill glass with cracked ice, shake and strain, fill with fizz [sic] water and serve.'

It's interesting that Grohusko's recipe calls for cider brandy rather than the more specific applejack, and that it references raspberry syrup over grenadine, which was then the darling modifier of the American bartending community. Perhaps most interesting of all is the addition of soda to the drink, directing it more towards the fizz family than the sour camp in which it resides today.

Possibly the most significant stage of the Jack Rose's otherwise mostly uneventful existence, and an occurrence that cemented its place in cocktail history, was its appearance in David A. Embury's seminal *The Fine Art of Mixing Drinks* (1948). Not only was Jack Rose included, but it was featured as one of Embury's 'Six Basic Drinks' alongside five far likelier candidates: Daiquiri, Manhattan, Martini, Side Car and Old Fashioned. That's a serious accolade from one of the most respected cocktail authors of all time.

Embury was a master at perfecting classic cocktails, and many of the recipes he penned remain the go-to formulae even today. Or perhaps his palate was just half a century ahead of its time? The Embury Jack Rose cuts back on citrus and grenadine, allowing the applejack to shine a little brighter.

# JAQUEMOT

50 ML / 1⅔ FL. OZ. JACKED-UP CIDER (*see opposite*)
20 ML / ⅔ FL. OZ. STRAINED LEMON JUICE
10 ML / ⅓ FL. OZ. FOREST FRUIT SYRUP • 15 ML / ½ FL. OZ. EGG WHITE

Shake all of the ingredients once with cubed ice, then strain and shake again with no ice to create a foamy head. Serve in a chilled Nick & Nora glass. No garnish needed… simply enjoy the taste of nature.

All this talk of freeze distillation makes me thirsty, and frankly it would be downright negligent of me not to have a go at freeze-distilling some applejack.

Fortunately, acquiring the base material for this endeavour wasn't a problem, as I live close to a cider producer in north Cornwall. Haywood Farm makes cider in the traditional manner, from around a dozen different apple varieties, pressed in a handmade wooden cider press and filtered through layers of hay. The juice is fermented and stored in oak barrels for a period of time. The owner of the farm is Tom, who has regularly plied me with cider over the years and hosted a number of parties on his farm. At least I think he has. The memories are somewhat hazy.

Freeze distillation can be done in your home freezer, but you will need to make plenty of space if you want to be left with a decent quantity of liquor at the end.

This is because freeze distillation is quite a wasteful way of getting from fermented product to spirit-strength hooch. It's inevitable that some of your alcohol will become trapped amongst frozen water and this will keep happening on each subsequent freeze/thaw.

Having said all of that, it really does work.

You will want to buy a floating alcometer to test the strength of your applejack, but remember to do this when your liquid is at room temperature (20°C/68°F) otherwise the reading will be wrong.

If I'm putting all this effort into the applejack, it seems a shame to skimp on the grenadine. For my Jaquemot I'm using a homemade raspberry and blackberry syrup to sweeten it. That natural synergy between dark forest fruits and orchard fruit plays nicely in to the overriding theme of autumn and the traditional practice of preserving flavours for wintertime enjoyment.

## FOREST FRUIT SYRUP

500 ML / 17 FL. OZ. WATER • 150 G / 5¼ OZ. RASPBERRIES
100 G / 3½ OZ. BLACKBERRIES • 30 G / 1 OZ. CRUSHED HAZELNUTS
2 G / 1/16 OZ. SALT • 500 G / 1 LB. 2 OZ. SUGAR

*Makes 1 litre/quart*

Add all of the ingredients except the sugar to a ziplock or sous vide bag. Cook in a water bath set to 60°C/140°F for 4 hours. Strain the liquor and sweeten with the sugar while still hot.

# JACKED-UP CIDER

5 LITRES/QUARTS STRONG FARMHOUSE CIDER (*the stronger the better*)

5 litres/5¼ quarts of cider at 7 per cent ABV contains 350 ml/12 fl. oz. of pure alcohol. To produce a spirit of 40 per cent ABV we will need to concentrate our 5 litre/quart batch down to 875 ml/30 fl. oz. of liquid. I'd like mine to be a little stronger than that, as I'll be popping it in an oak barrel for a few weeks to mature, so let's call it 900 ml/30½ fl. oz. of liquid.

Clear enough space in your freezer to accommodate a 5-litre/5¼-quart plastic container. Ideally your container will have a screw cap and be able to stand up, but any plastic container will do. Fill it with cider but fit the lid loosely to avoid

the container breaking when the liquid expands during freezing.

Once frozen, remove the container from the freezer and take off the lid. If you used a container with a screw cap, simply turn it upside down and place in a 2-litre/quart jug/pitcher to defrost. A large colander will also work. The liquid that leaches out first will have a relatively high alcoholic strength and will slowly decrease over time as lower-strength liquid thaws.

Once you've collected about 2 litres/quarts, discard the rest of the ice and prepare to repeat the process again.

For the second freeze/thaw you will be looking to collect 900 ml/30½ fl. oz. of liquid, which should produce a spirit of approximately 40 per cent ABV. You can test this with an alcometer, or put the liquid back in the freezer. If it doesn't freeze, it means you're nearing spirit strength. If it does, you need to repeat the process again!

Once you have produced enough applejack to fill a small oak cask (see page 53), pop it in the barrel and taste it periodically until you're happy with the results.

For a new 3-litre/quart barrel a couple of weeks should be sufficient maturing time.

# PISCO SOUR

50 ML/1⅔ FL. OZ. MACCHU PISCO
25 ML/¾ FL. OZ. LIME JUICE
12.5 ML/½ FL. OZ. SUGAR SYRUP (*see page 32*)
½ AN EGG WHITE
A FEW DASHES ANGOSTURA BITTERS

Shake all of the ingredients (except the bitters) with cubed ice. Strain the ice out of the shaker, then dry shake (with no ice) to whip more air into the foam. Pour into a rocks glass and finish with a few dashes of Angostura bitters.

Importing wine and spirits into the New World was a long-winded and expensive exercise, so colonies in North America began to produce genever and whisky from domestically grown cereals. In the Caribbean, where sugarcane flourished, it was rum that flowed from the stills. Meanwhile, in Pacific South America, grapes were better suited to the climate, so they made wine and pisco.

Depending of whether you're from Chile or Peru, you'll likely have a different take on which nation pisco originates from. The same will also be true of the Pisco Sour, which is the signature serve for this particular spirit. The sour family of cocktails goes right back to Jerry Thomas' *Bar-Tender's Guide* (1862) and can trace its origins back further still, to the sweet and sour punches of the 18th century.

The first reference to a cocktail that sounds like a Pisco Sour comes from *Nuevo Manual de Cocina a la Criolla* ('The New Manual of Creole Cusine'), which was published in Lima, Peru, in 1903. Written in Spanish, the book includes a recipe for a drink that is titled simply Cocktail:

'An egg white, a glass of Pisco, a teaspoon of fine sugar, and a few drops of lime as desired, this will open your appetite. Up to three glasses can be made with one egg white and a heaping teaspoon of fine sugar, adding the rest of the ingredients as needed for each glass. All this is beaten in a cocktail shaker until you've made a small punch.'

This certainly sounds like a Pisco Sour, although it is missing the all-important Angostura bitters, which are ritualistically dashed over the foamy top of the cocktail.

That next, crucial step was probably taken by Victor Morris, an expat American businessman who moved to Peru in the same year that *Nuevo Manual de Cocina a la Criolla* was printed. Morris worked for the Cerro de Pasco Railroad until 1915. The following year, he took quite a change in direction, opening Morris' Bar in Lima in 1916.

The bar became a popular hangout for the Peruvian upper classes (people like José Lindley, the English founder of Inca Kola) as well as English-speaking expats. Some say that Morris was the first to use Angostura bitters in the drink, while others credit Mario Bruiget, a Peruvian bartender who worked for Morris in the 1920s. Either way, the Pisco Sour is a delicious drink.

In fact, it may be the best iteration of the sour family going. There's something about the untamed, winey characteristics of pisco that works very well with lime. Where most spirits fight the acidity and become a little neutered, pisco seems to thrive off it, becoming emboldened by that silky egg-white texture.

If any further proof of its genius is required, let me tell you this: in all my years working in bars, it was the Whisky Sour that was the most called-for member of the sour family. But it was the Pisco Sour that got those in the know the most excited.

This is a cult drink.

# TIGER'S MILK

40 ML/1⅓ FL. OZ. LA DIABLADA PISCO • 40 ML/1⅓ FL. OZ. QUINOA MILK
20 ML/⅔ FL. OZ. KEY LIME *or* REGULAR LIME JUICE • 5 ML/1 TEASPOON SUGAR SYRUP
2 G/1⁄16 OZ. LEMON BALM LEAVES (*approx.* 15 LEAVES) • 4 G/⅛ OZ. KATSUOBUSHI FLAKES
1 G/4 PINCHES CHOPPED CHILLI/CHILE (*pick one that suits your taste*) • 0.5 G/2 PINCHES SALT

Add all of the ingredients to a cocktail shaker and leave to infuse for a minute. Add cubed ice, then shake well for 10 seconds. Double-strain into a chilled clay pot or rocks glass. I garnished this drink with the leftover stalk of a bunch of grapes, to reflect the base material of the pisco, because it finds a use for something that would otherwise go straight in the bin/trash, and because, quite frankly, it looks amazing.

Tiger's Milk (aka Leche de Tigre) is a popular Peruvian hangover drink made from of the run-off juices from a ceviche marinade. To refresh your memory, ceviche is Peru's most famous dish, made by curing fresh fish in a mixture of citrus juice, chilli/chile, onion, salt and pepper, along with any other ingredients that the chef sees fit to use. Of course this makes for some fantastic-tasting fish, but also leaves a fair bit of fishy-flavoured marinade lying around. If you're feeling the effects of too much pisco consumption the night before, and if Peruvians are to be believed, Tiger's Milk is a miracle cure.

The only problem is, no two Peruvians can agree on what goes into Tiger's Milk. Everything from fresh apple and ginger, through to umami-rich stocks and dehydrated scallops have featured as ingredients. Most people agree that Tiger's Milk can only be made by a Peruvian, while others state that only a fisherman from the Chorillos region of Lima has the skill to do it properly. What most Peruvians do agree upon is that proper Tiger's Milk should be cold, sour and rejuvenating… which doesn't place the drink too far from a Pisco Sour, so why not mash the two drinks together?

My recipe uses katsuobushi (dried Japanese tuna) in place of fresh fish. This was a strategy I picked up from the late Toshiro Konishi, a Japanese chef who was an early pioneer of Peruvian–Japanese fusion cuisine, which subsequently became a global sensation. Because the tuna is smoked during its preparation, it gives a subtle smoky quality to the drink without being overly fishy.

Some Peruvians advocate the use of cow's milk in the production of Tiger's Milk. I'm using store-bought quinoa milk instead. Why quinoa? Well, because quinoa originates from Peru and was first farmed there some 4,000 years ago. Why store-bought? Because store-bought, packaged quinoa milk tends to contain gelling agents, which thicken and stabilise the drink, alleviating the need to use egg white in my cocktail.

For a fresh herbal kick, I'm also including lemon balm, which is the chief flavour of Inca Kola – Peru's most popular soda. For the citrus component I'm using key lime, which is smaller and seedier than the Persian limes that we get in UK supermarkets. They also have a stronger aroma and a higher acidity, and a thick yellow-coloured rind when ripe – though they're often picked when green. Although their name comes from the Florida Keys (where the variety was naturalised), key limes are grown all over Central and South America. They are the only Peruvian citrus fruit that is grown all year round. You can use regular limes if you wish, though.

The citrus is balanced by both sugar and salt, which will elevate the herbal and fruity notes of the cocktail and add depth to the katsuobushi. For added piquancy I also use fresh chilli/chile.

The Peruvian culture of ceviche requires that ingredients are fresh and prepared quickly. Although there are lots of ingredients in this drink, unlike some of my other creations, this cocktail can be built directly in the shaker.

# VODKA

# WHITE RUSSIAN

40 ML / 1⅓ FL. OZ. BELVEDERE VODKA
20 ML / ⅔ FL. OZ. COFFEE LIQUEUR (*try* CONKER)
20 ML / ⅔ FL. OZ. DOUBLE/HEAVY CREAM

You can shake or stir this one, but I prefer to build it in the glass to avoid the foamy top.
Add all of the ingredients to a rocks glass and stir for a minute with plenty of cubed ice.

The White Russian is not a cocktail for everyone. It's a drink that underwent periods of huge popularity in the 1970s and again in the late 1990s, thanks largely to the The Dude in *The Big Lebowski*, who spends most of the movie mixing White Russians or drinking them (nine in total, though one of them ends up on the floor).

At the time of writing, however, the White Russian has fallen out of favour. Sickly coffee liqueur, anonymous vodka and gloopy cream are not appealing ingredients to a generation of drinkers that question provenance, sustainability and calorific content. Truth is, a White Russian is the drink uncool people order thinking that it makes them look cool. So like a shell suit or a lava lamp, perhaps it's time to unceremoniously load it into the back of a people carrier and send if off to the place where cocktails go to die.

But before we condemn the White Russian to the great plughole in the sky, it's worth highlighting two surprising things about this drink. The first is its history: there are 750 recipes in Harry Craddock's seminal 1930 work *The Savoy Cocktail Book*, but just four of them use vodka. Of those four recipes, two of them are drinks that contain crème de cacao. And of those two drinks one of them, called Barbara, contains vodka, crème de cacao and cream. Not quite a White Russian, of course – it's missing the all-important coffee liqueur – but not far off. Barbara was inspired by Alexander, which was originally a gin-based drink that first appeared in Hugo Ensslin's 1916 book *Recipes for Mixed Drinks*.

Coffee liqueur was first introduced to the commercial market in 1936, when Kahlúa was launched. It took some years for it to percolate its way into a cocktail glass, the evidence of which appears in *The Stork Club Bar Book*

of 1946, which lists another riff on the Barbara theme, named Alexander the Great. This drink combines crème de cacao, coffee liqueur, vodka and cream – a chocolate White Russian, if you will.

Logic would suggest that in the next part of the story somebody removed the crème de cacao and changed the name to White Russian? Well, not exactly.

Remember there were two vodka drinks containing chocolate liqueur in *The Savoy Cocktail Book*? Well, the other one (not Barbara) was called the Russian Cocktail. This drink comprised equal parts vodka, gin and crème de cacao. It's a terrible drink, but it has a strong claim to being the precursor of the Black Russian (remove the gin and switch the crème de cacao for coffee liqueur), which was invented in 1949. The drink's inventor, Gustave Tops, who worked at the Hotel Metropole in Brussels, created this signature drink (comprising two parts vodka and one part Kahlúa) for Perle Mesta, the American ambassador to Luxembourg, who was hanging out in the bar.

As we move in to the 1960s, Alexander the Great and the Black Russian (this is beginning to sound like an epic saga) converged and the White Russian was born. The first mention of it can be found in California's *Oakland Tribune* on 21 November 1965. It featured in an advert for Southern Comfort's short-lived coffee liqueur, and the recipe called for '1 oz. each [of] Southern, vodka, cream.'

With the history part out of the way, I guess you'll be wanting to know what the second interesting thing about a White Russian is? Well, here it is: it tastes great! Sweet coffee, unctuous cream and a nice boozy kick. What's not to like?!

# WHITE RUSSIAN LIQUEUR CHOCOLATES

200 g/7 oz. White Chocolate • ½ Vanilla Pod/Bean
170 g/6 oz. single/light Cream • 200 g/7 oz. Dark/Bittersweet
Chocolate (minimum 70% Cocoa) • 35 ml/1¼ fl. oz. Vodka
35 ml/1¼ fl. oz. Espresso (*or very strong coffee*) • 50 g/1¾ oz. Softened Butter

Coffee, cream and booze sounds as much like a delicious dessert to me as it does a cocktail – tiramisu, anyone? It got me thinking about liqueur chocolates and how terrible most are. The cheap ones are too sweet and sickly and the expensive ones are filled with too much poor-quality booze.

In defence of the expensive ones, it's not the fault of the chocolate itself per se, but a problem with us humans. Most of us can handle a shot of spirit in its liquid form because we've trained our palates to approach it cautiously. But things turn nasty when you mix that shot in with the act of chewing. During normal mastication we don't generally encounter alcohol, because solid stuff is rarely ever alcoholic. So most of us go about or daily business, chewing with careless disregard, safe in the knowledge that most solid things aren't hiding any surprises. But throw a measure of hard liquor into your sandwich-filled mouth and you'll get quite a surprise unless you rein in your chew. The same can be said for a liquor-filled chocolate, which requires that you chew it, then punishes you when you do. You can't win.

I think the trick here is to dial the alcohol down to a manageable level, while maintaining the kick and, most importantly of all, delivering on flavour and balance.

My White Russian Liqueur Chocolates comprise two components: the shell, made from tempered white chocolate, and the centre, which is filled with a boozy, coffee-flavoured dark/bittersweet chocolate ganache.

These are easy to make, assuming you have a few important pieces of equipment. First and foremost are chocolate moulds. Take your pick of the various shapes available, but be sure to use one made from silicone that has at least a 20 ml/⅔ fl. oz. volume to it. You will also need a palette knife for scraping off excess chocolate, a temperature probe, wire rack, whisk, piping/pastry bag and steel bowl or bain-marie.

First, temper the white chocolate by gently melting 120 g/4¼ oz. of it in a bain-marie or steel bowl placed above a pan of steaming water. Keep stirring, and once the chocolate reaches 45–50°C/113–122°F, take it off the heat and throw in the remaining white chocolate along with the the seeds from the vanilla pod/bean. When all of the chocolate is melted and glossy, pour it into the mould, ensuring all parts of it are filled. Place a tray under the wire rack and place the mould upside down on the rack so that the chocolate falls back out of the mould.

Next, heat the cream to 80°C/176°F and set to one side to cool. Temper the dark/bittersweet chocolate the same way you did with the white chocolate. Once tempered, slowly beat the warm cream into the chocolate one splash at a time. Once fully incorporated, add the vodka and the espresso and continue to beat the mixture. Finally, add the butter and stir until everything is incorporated.

While the ganache cools, turn your chocolate mould back over and scrape off any excess chocolate with a palette knife. Transfer your cooled ganache to a piping/pastry bag and pipe a dollop into each of the moulds, being careful not to overfill.

Melt the excess white chocolate that you caught in the tray back up to 40°C/104°F, then pour this over your mould to seal in the ganache. Use the palette knife to spread the melted chocolate, ensuring that any bubbles are removed from the mould.

Allow your chocolates to set for a further 2 hours, then transfer to the fridge. They should keep for at least a month, but I challenge you to resist them for that long!

# BULLSHOT

....................................................................................

400 G/14 OZ. CAMPBELL'S BEEF BROTH
150 ML/5 FL. OZ. BELVEDERE UNFILTERED VODKA
150 ML/5 FL. OZ. WATER • 30 ML/1 FL. OZ. LEMON JUICE • TABASCO (*to taste*)

*Makes 4*

Mix everything together in a jug/pitcher and pour over cubed ice in a rocks glass. Give it
a brief stir. If you wish, you can also experiment with other ingredients familiar to Bloody
Mary: Worcester/Worcestershire Sauce, pepper, sherry etc.

If you're a fan of the Bloody Mary but always found it a touch too… *vegetarian* for your tastes, the Bullshot might be the meaty upgrade you've been searching for. As the name suggests, the Bullshot contains beef, or more specifically, beef broth. When does a cocktail cease being a cocktail and become simply beef stock with a splash of vodka in it? Well, right about now if you ask me, but given the bizarre level of popularity that the Bullshot enjoyed in the middle of the 20th century, it's difficult to argue against its status as a paid-up, card-carrying cocktail.

And how is such a drink conceived in the first place, you may ask? Not through the actions of a veterinary surgeon, I hasten to add, but through the ingenuity of a certain restaurant operator from Detroit.

The year was 1952 and Lester Gruber's London Chop House (LCH) was not only one of the most popular restaurants in Motor City, but ranked as one of the best restaurants in the whole of North America. Frequented by celebrities like Aretha Franklin and barons from Detroit's booming motor industry, including Henry Ford II, LCH was *the place* to be seen eating and drinking. Drinks were not only of the carnivorous kind, mind you. The legendary LCH Pick-Up Drinks menu ran 9–11 every morning and included Old Pepper (rye whiskey, bourbon, hot sauces) and Kilroy's Bracer (Cognac, egg, anise) among its stimulants.

By the early 1950s, the place was so busy that Gruber opened a spillover bar across the road, called Caucus Club. And it was in this bar that Gruber became acquainted with John Hurley, a Don Draper-esque PR exec who was, at that time, fretting over a million cans of Campbell's Beef Broth that weren't flying off the shelves. At this time vodka was rapidly becoming the most popular drink in America, and Americans never grew tired of marvelling at how it could turn literally any liquid into an alcoholic one without altering the flavour of the original liquid. Beef broth was no exception.

The drink – served on the rocks with a twist of lemon – was known under various headings before Bullshot was settled on. Soup on the Rocks was one such moniker that was even marketed by Campbell's itself, albeit without the vodka (Campbell's was something of a family-friendly company). Other rejected titles included Ox on the Rocks and Matador. I would have gone for The Bovine Comedy.

In 1957, the Heublein Corporation, then owners of Smirnoff Vodka, got a hold of the drink and were running adverts in *Esquire* magazine for The Vodka Drink with Beef In It. By the early 1960s the Bullshot was no bullshit, and had shot to international fame. The drink caught on in part because it was so left-field – enjoyed by those so cool that they could afford to be a little odd. Beef broth was also deemed to be a bit of a superfood back then. One *New York Post* journalist remarked that the drink was 'full of vitamins'.

It took a few decades before people realised that salty beef broth was not going to grant everlasting youth after all and that no amount of vodka was likely to change that. By then, however, the Bullshot had already 'steak'd' its place in the history books.

....................................................................................

# UMAMI BOMB

40 ML/1⅓ FL. OZ. BELVEDERE VODKA
10 ML/⅓ FL. OZ. AMONTILLADO SHERRY
150 ML/5 FL. OZ. UMAMI STOCK (*see opposite*)

Build the ingredients straight into a rocks glass filled with cubed ice. Give a good stir,
then spritz the oils from some yuzu zest over the top and discard the peel.

Though it might not be to everyone's taste, there's an undeniable neatness to combining your pre-dinner aperitif with the first course of your dinner. As with most savoury cocktails though, the Bullshot is more of an appetite suppressant than a stimulant. For most of us, all that concentrated savouriness will dispel any ideas of solid foodstuffs altogether.

But if it's a 'liquid dinner' that you're after, a drink such as the Bullshot might not be a bad option. Watching your waistline but fancy a drink? Try a Bullshot: it's relatively low in carbohydrates and sugars, and generally doesn't contain many calories besides the alcohol. Indeed, a standard-sized Bullshot, as listed in the previous recipe, contains just 118 calories and over 90 per cent of that can be attributed to the vodka. Could the Bullshot be the next health drink? Probably not, and certainly not in a society that is becoming increasingly wise to the negative health associations with the consumption of meat and meat products (not to mention their environmental impact).

But the idea of a cocktail that satisfies with salt and savoury, rather than sweet and sour, is not a bad one. The Bloody Mary is, of course, not far off the mark here, but relies quite heavily on the savoury properties of tomato juice for my liking, which varies enormously in quality.

To get to true savoury pleasure we're far better off looking at Asian cuisine and the umami-rich stocks and soups that feature heavily on menus. Whether it's dashi, miso, soy sauce, mushrooms, nori or wakame (a popular sea vegetable grown in Japan since the 8th century), all of these vegetarian ingredients share the same rich and powerful umami flavours. That's why there's every opportunity to create an indulgent, savoury cocktail that has all the flavour of a Bullshot, only it's more concentrated, more refined, and better for you!

This drink asks you to make a light savoury stock with just a hint of saltiness. I'm also mixing in a touch of Amontillado sherry, which will bolster that savoury flavour with nuttiness and also add some soft, dried-fruit flavours into the mix. The rye-based vodka adds a peppery seasoning.

# UMAMI STOCK

1 LITRE/QUART WATER
10 G/⅓ OZ. CRUSHED KOMBU
50 G/1¾ OZ. DRIED MUSHROOMS
20 G/¾ OZ. WHITE MISO PASTE
0.5 G/A PINCH XANTHAN GUM
2 G/1/16 OZ. SALT
15 G/½ OZ. MIRIN

Boil half of the water in a pan and add the kombu and the mushrooms. Leave to steep for 30 minutes, then strain and reserve. While the mixture is steeping, mix the miso paste, xanthan, salt and mirin in a medium-sized bowl, along with a splash of the water, and blitz thoroughly with an immersion (stick) blender. Continue adding the remaining water, blending out any lumps as you go. Mix in your strained kombu/mushroom water, then bottle and refrigerate (the mixture will keep for a week).

# BLUE LAGOON

30 ML/1 FL. OZ. BELVEDERE VODKA • 20 ML/⅔ FL. OZ. BOLS BLUE CURAÇAO
15 ML/½ FL. OZ. LIME JUICE • SAN PELLEGRINO LIMONATA (LEMONADE)

Add the first three ingredients to a highball glass filled with ice and stir for 30 seconds.
Top up with more ice, then stir through the lemonade to fill the glass.
Garnish with a slice of orange.

Blue cocktails should really only be consumed in horizontal positions. They're kitsch, ridiculous and tend to be a lot of fun – ironically, not at all 'blue'. Blue drinks also have the potential to be quite delicious. Some people are surprised at this, and that's because they don't know what to make of blue as a flavour. We'll discuss that more in my True Blue cocktail (see pages 90–1) but first let's take a look at the bluest drink of them all – the Blue Lagoon.

The secret to this drink's colour is of course the blue Curaçao. Curaçao is an island in the Caribbean, off the coast of Venezuela. The island's name comes from the Portuguese word for 'healing', which came about after sailors who had contracted scurvy (vitamin C deficiency) ate the fruit of the island and made miraculous recoveries. The Spanish introduced the Valencia orange to the island in the early 16th century, but it shrivelled, turned green and fell off the tree unripe in the dry Caribbean heat. This new orange (*Citrus aurantium currassuviencis*) became known locally as 'Laraha' and since it was too bitter to be eaten, it was used to make aromatic oils and liqueurs. Dutch colonists began to occupy Curaçao in the 1630s after the Dutch Republic declared independence from Spain. They brought the liqueur to Europe and called it Curaçao.

Nobody knows why blue Curaçao came into existence, but Bols Blue Curaçao had arrived in the US prior to Prohibition in the 1920s. There is evidence suggesting Bols sold various other colours of Curaçao at one time or another, indicating that blue was not the chosen colour, but just one colour among many. It happened to be the one that stuck, though.

By the 1950s, Bols had stepped up their sales strategy, expanding Blue Curaçao into the European market and selling it as a cocktail ingredient in the US. That's presumably what the Hawaii sales representative from Bols thought when he asked Harry Yee, the head bartender at the Hilton Hawaiian Village Waikiki, to design a blue cocktail in 1957. The subsequent Blue Hawaiian contained vodka, rum, blue Curaçao, pineapple juice, citrus and sugar. A more fitting name would have been Green Hawaiian, because mixing pineapple juice (which is yellow) with blue Curaçao (blue) gives you a green drink. Nice try, Mr Yee.

Around the same time, but on the other side of the Atlantic, Andy MacElhone (son of legendary bartender Harry MacElhone) developed a drink at Harry's New York Bar in Paris using the newly launched Blue Curaçao. MacElhone's drink was unmistakably blue, seeing as all the ingredients except the Curaçao were clear: gin, vodka, lemonade, lime juice, sugar. He called the drink Blue Lagoon.

Despite its gaudy appearance and daft name, the Blue Lagoon is in fact a perfectly tasty drink. The flavours here are all about citrus, with the holy trinity of orange, lemon and lime. The Blue Lagoon is similar to the Cosmopolitan in this way, confusing you with strange colour but in the simplest sense delivering a medley of citrus flavours. The beauty of a drink like this is how forgiving it can be, and how easily it can be customised to your tastes. You can adjust the quantity of lime juice to balance the sweetness, or select a lemonade that has a decent, puckering acidity, and do away with the lime and sugar altogether if you like.

# TRUE BLUE

. . . . . . . . . . . . . . . . . . . . . . . . . . . . . . . . . . . . . . . . . . . . . . . . . . .

50 ML / 1⅔ FL. OZ. BELVEDERE VODKA
50 ML / 1⅔ FL. OZ. BLUE RASPBERRY SHRUB (*see opposite*)
100 ML / 3½ FL. OZ. SODA WATER

Stir the vodka and the shrub over cubed ice.
Strain into a chilled highball glass and top up with ice-cold soda water.

Blue drinks are an enigma. What makes them so diabolically desirable? Where does blue colouring come from? And most importantly: what does blue actually taste like?

Look around you. There are very few naturally occurring blue plants. You get the blue poppy, butterfly pea, and blue gentians, but many of the flowers that have blue in their names are in fact violet or purple (I'm looking at you, bluebell). Then there's blueberries, which aren't exactly blue either – more of a dusty indigo. When our brains attempt to determine the flavour of blue food or drink we tend to fall back on the only blue things we've ever actually put in our mouths: confectionery and mouthwash.

In the world of confectionery, colour is extremely important because it communicates the anticipated flavour of the product to one of the most stubborn groups of tasters there is – children. In the Western world, yellow is lemon, red is strawberry (or cherry), white is vanilla, orange is orange, green is apple (or lime), and purple is blackcurrant. Be prepared to face the wrath of a child if you dare to tamper with these rules.

Because we encounter these colour and flavour combinations as children and because most of the colours mentioned are the colours of the fruits that occur naturally, the associations become powerfully ingrained into our minds and are surprisingly resistant to alteration (it would take perhaps years of eating yellow-coloured strawberry candy/sweets to build a crossmodal relationship between the two).

One study in 2010, led by Mayu Shankar in the Department of Experimental Psychology at the University of Oxford, found that young British participants associated the colour blue with the flavour of raspberry, while young Chinese participants associated it with mint. So the expected flavour of blue does vary by culture. In the West, the raspberry flavour of blue probably came about as a design consideration intended to distinguish it from red, strawberry-flavoured confectionery and some soft drinks continue to follow this convention.

Not all blue confectionery is raspberry flavoured, however. In 1995 M&M's launched a blue-coloured candy after a public vote to choose the next colour in the range. Smarties launched a blue version of their candy in 1988. When they pulled it in 2006 (due to a lack of natural blue food colouring) many people believed the decision was made because the blue colouring caused hyperactivity in children. The blue colouring that Smarties used was found to have no links to hyperactivity, so the association probably came from the simple 'unnaturalness' of the colour or maybe even the colour's association with electricity!

In my experience 'blue raspberry' flavoured products taste nothing like raspberry at all. This might be because they're not red and the crossmodal connections between blue and raspberry are simply not robust enough for my brain to establish a link.

Blue-coloured soft drinks don't tend to use natural raspberry flavours though, so they tend to lack the whole kaleidoscope of rounded fruitiness that the berry has. Raspberries are delicious, so I set out to make a blue-coloured raspberry infusion that could feature in a Blue Lagoon cocktail.

. . . . . . . . . . . . . . . . . . . . . . . . . . . . . . . . . . . . . . . . . . . . . . . . . . .

# BLUE RASPBERRY SHRUB

700 ML/23½ FL. OZ. SHERRY VINEGAR • 500 G/1 LB. 2 OZ. FRESH RASPBERRIES
2 G/1⁄16 OZ. AGAR • 150 ML/5 FL. OZ. COLD WATER
200 G/7 OZ. SUGAR • 2 G/1⁄16 OZ. SALT
NATURAL BLUE FOOD COLOURING

*Makes approximately 500 ml/17 fl. oz.*

To get this drink a rich shade of blue, you will need to clarify the shrub using the techniques detailed on pages 46–8. Please note that we won't come close to perfectly clarifying this shrub, but knocking back some of the pink hue will keep your finished liquid on the blue side of purple.

Put the vinegar and raspberries in a ziplock bag and drop it into a 50°C/122°F water bath for 2 hours. Once infused, strain the raspberries out of the vinegar and reserve the liquid. Next, mix the agar and cold water in a large pan and bring to the boil, giving it a good whisk while it heats. Now pour the strained vinegar into the agar solution and whisk it together. Pop the pan in the fridge and wait for it to set. Then follow the instructions for clarification filtering on pages 46–8. Add the sugar and salt, then stir in the colouring until you achieve your desired level of blue (remembering that the drink will be diluted with soda water).

# VODKA MARTINI

. . . . . . . . . . . . . . . . . . . . . . . . . . . . . . . . . . . . . . . . . . . . . .

50 ML/1⅔ FL. OZ. BELVEDERE VODKA
10 ML/⅓ FL. OZ. DRY VERMOUTH

Stir both ingredients over ice for at least 90 seconds. Strain into a frozen Martini glass. Garnish with a spritz of lemon and discard the peel afterwards. I hate having lemon peel floating around in my Martini glass. It gets in the way and causes the second half of the drink to taste entirely of lemon. Don't do it!

At the turn of the 20th century, any American who had heard of vodka considered it a peasant's drink. *The Spatula*, a journal for pharmacists, wrote in 1905 '[that] the same kind of drink can be "enjoyed" by drinking the deadly spirits used in alcohol lamps'. It went on to conclude that '[vodka] may suit the Muscovite for the dead of winter, but in a climate like ours it could never become popular'. How wrong they were.

The first written reference to a vodka cocktail occurred in 1903, published in a New York–based Democratic periodical journal called *The Tammany Times*, where a fictional drunk Russian fisherman called Rumsouranwhisky engages with and destroys an imaginary Japanese fleet 'after soakin' in a couple train oil an' vodka cocktails to steady his nerve'. But since train oil (whale blubber) hardly counts as an ingredient, we'll revert to the first proper vodka cocktail, which made its entrance on the menu at the St Charles Hotel in New Orleans in 1911. Aptly named Russian Cocktail, this drink consisted of three parts vodka to two parts Russian cherry liqueur, and appeared in a little-known cocktail book called *Beverage Deluxe* in the same year.

Despite token mentions in a handful of other cocktail books, vodka maintained a vague yet fierce reputation up until the post–World War II period. Things would change quickly, though, as between 1950 and 1955 the quantity imported into the US increased from 50,000 cases to 5 million cases. Gin and whiskey were reliable spirits of an older generation, but easily substituted for this cool 'new' Cold War-era spirit. The Martini cocktail was near the front of the queue/line for this treatment.

The first reference to a Vodka Martini is in David A. Embury's *The Fine Art of Mixing Drinks* (1948) in which Embury offers a recipe for a Vodka Medium Martini, mixed with both French and Italian vermouth and apricot brandy. Embury mentions that vodka can be substituted for gin in a classic Martini, at which point you have a Vodka Martini.

In Ted Saucier's 1951 book *Bottoms Up*, the same drink goes under the guise of a Vodkatini and calls for '4/5 jigger Smirnoff vodka [and] 1/5 jigger dry vermouth', with a twist of lemon peel as a garnish. In later editions of *The Fine Art of Mixing Drinks*, Embury refers to the same Vodka Martini as a Kangaroo, which still gets bandied about today, though nobody has worked out where the link to the marsupial comes from.

However, the 1950s literature that had a bigger influence over the Vodka Martini's rise to fame was found in the fiction section. James Bond is synonymous with the Vodka Martini, and while he didn't do the drink any harm, the movie adaptations hugely overstate Bond's attachment for the drink. Bond was a heavy drinker, but his preference was more towards whisky and Champagne than vodka. That said, he drinks neat Wolfschmidt vodka with M in *Moonraker* (1955), where he drops black pepper into the glass, stating that, 'In Russia, where you get a lot of bathtub liquor, it's an understood thing to sprinkle a little pepper in your glass. It takes the fusel oil to the bottom.'

In the first Bond novel, *Casino Royale* (1953), Bond famously asks the bartender to mix a Vesper Martini (comprising gin, vodka and Kina Lillet) but he drinks his first true Vodka Martini in the second novel *Live & Let Die* (1954), in which Fleming handily provides the recipe at the end of the book (six parts vodka to one part vermouth, shaken).

. . . . . . . . . . . . . . . . . . . . . . . . . . . . . . . . . . . . . . . . . . . . . .

# EXPLODED VODKA MARTINI

50 ml / 1⅔ fl. oz. Belvedere Single-Estate Rye Vodka
10 ml / ⅓ fl. oz. Gancia Bianco Vermouth
5 ml / 1 teaspoon High-Pressure Hydrosol (*see opposite*)

Add all of the ingredients to a mixing beaker filled with cubed ice.
Stir for 90 seconds, then strain into a chilled tulip glass. No garnish.

My second bar – Worship Street Whistling Shop – opened on 29 April 2011, the date of Prince William and Kate Middleton's wedding. Though unintentional, it seemed a fitting date, as our 120-capacity venue was styled like a Victorian-era gin shop. Queen Victoria's long reign (1837–1901) was a period of enormous industrial, cultural and political evolution, but it was also a time of great change in drinking habits, when the punches of the Georgian period morphed into cocktails. Whistling Shop was a celebration of that time.

Despite most of the cocktails on the first menu being classic in their formulae, all were embellished with modern, innovative flourishes that set them apart from the norm (much like this book). More often than not, these innovations had a 'crackpot' kind of feel to them, and we wanted our guests to feel as though they were experiencing Frankenstein's lab, or exploring the mind of Sherlock Holmes. One cocktail on the list was 'irradiated', another contained 'removed cream'. The whole experience was intended to be hairbrained, a little confusing, but most of all fun.

Much of the development work was done by Ryan Chetiyawardana, who at the time was employed as our bar manager, but has since opened his own award-winning venues (and published a couple of books). Ryan had a knack for taking murky historical drink concepts and turning them into real drinks that actually taste good. The Exploded Vodka Martini was his drink. The cocktail had no direct correlation to a drink from the Victorian period but instead celebrated the work of some of the era's engineering greats: Edison, Stephenson, Faraday... not to mention Aeneas Coffey, the inventor of the continuous still.

The construction of the cocktail is simple because it contains just three ingredients: vodka, dry vermouth and a water-based distillation (hydrosol) infused with coriander seed, black pepper and sarsaparilla. Under normal circumstances you can make a hydrosol using any type of still and the process is similar to that of producing a gin, except plain water is used instead of neutral spirit. But for this drink we were interested in extracting the difficult-to-access earthy flavours of hard spices, the kind of flavours that normally only manifest over long, high-temperature cooking. The hope was that these rich spices would pair well with the rye characteristics of Belvedere vodka.

Operating a still at normal temperatures (where water boils at 100°C/212°F), we found the system didn't have enough energy to claim those deep, spicy flavours. It was at this point that Ryan came up with the idea of converting a pressure cooker into a still (like you do).

The boiling point of any liquid is determined by the ambient atmospheric pressure: the higher the ambient pressure, the higher the boiling point of the liquid. Most pressure cookers max out at 1 bar above atmospheric pressure, which raises the boiling point of water to 121°C/250°F. When the goal is to extract lots of flavour, that extra 21°C/70°F goes a long way, unlocking doors and granting access to additional taste compounds on the aromatic spectrum. All pressure cookers have a release valve that opens up once you hit max pressure, releasing a plume of vapour. By directing the vapour through an upturned glass funnel connected to a condenser, we were able to capture a liquid with unprecedented botanical richness. It was a ghetto set-up to say the least. We called it the 'kaboom-still'.

# HIGH-PRESSURE HYDROSOL

1 LITRE/QUART WATER
200 G/7 OZ. CORIANDER SEEDS
100 G/3½ OZ. WHOLE BLACK PEPPERCORNS
100 G/3½ OZ. SARSAPARILLA ROOT

Any form of distillation will do an adequate job of extracting the flavour of these products, but for best results use the pressure-cooker method. I use a clamp stand to hold everything in place, and connect an upturned funnel to plastic tubing that connects to a glass condenser unit. A small aquarium pump submerged in a bowl of icy water is perfect for chilling the condenser. Position your pressure cooker so the release valve sits directly underneath the funnel. Add all the ingredients, seal the lid in place, then turn the heat up to the max. As the distillate condenses, collect in a glass and store in the fridge until you're ready to use it.

# LONG ISLAND ICED TEA

25 ML/¾ FL. OZ. BELVEDERE VODKA
25 ML/¾ FL. OZ. DON JULIO BLANCO TEQUILA
25 ML/¾ FL. OZ. BEEFEATER GIN
25 ML/¾ FL. OZ. APPLETON SIGNATURE RUM
25 ML/¾ FL. OZ. MERLET TRIPLE SEC
15 ML/½ FL. OZ. LEMON JUICE
COKE

Add everything but the Coke to a highball glass filled with ice. Give a good stir, mixing all of the ingredients thoroughly. Top up with more ice, then fill the glass with Coke. Garnish with a lemon wheel.

Here's a drink with no short measure of confusion surrounding it, which I guess is hardly surprising for a cocktail that contains five different base spirits.

When I first cut my teeth as a bartender, I was told that the Long Island was a Prohibition-era drink. The inference being that it looked liked iced tea and was called iced tea, despite being most assuredly an alcoholic beverage that happened to contain no tea at all. It was easy to imagine cops raiding a neighbourhood bar in New York's Long Island, and to their dismay discovering everyone sipping from tall glasses of what appeared to be iced tea.

This idea of an illicit, Prohibition-themed story behind the creation of the Long Island Iced Tea was later reaffirmed for me by the story of Old Man Bishop. This resident of Long Island, Tennessee, created a drink in the 1920s called – wait for it – Old Man Bishop that included rum, vodka, whiskey, gin, tequila, and maple syrup. It seemed to me that the origin story was all tied up.

But if you run a Google search asking 'Who invented the Long Island Iced Tea?', you're sure to encounter Robert 'Rosebud' Butt. This man claims to have come up with the cocktail in 1972 when working at the Oak Beach Inn on (of course) Long Island. He even has a website telling us so:

'I participated in a cocktail-creating contest. Triple Sec had to be included, and the bottles started flying.

My concoction was an immediate hit and quickly became the house drink at the Oak Beach Inn.'

Butt acknowledges that: 'Possibly similar concoctions were created elsewhere, at another time,' but what he doesn't acknowledge is *Betty Crocker's New Picture Cook Book*, published in 1961. This is where the first printed recipe for the Long Island Iced Tea can be found, and it was followed by appearances in the *American Home All-purpose Cookbook* of 1966 by Virginia T. Habeeb and in *Punch* in 1969. It seems Mr Butt might have been talking out of his… well, you get it.

As for the drink, the ingredients require little introduction. Coke and lemon juice, mixed with equal parts gin, rum, tequila, vodka and triple sec. Nearly everyone squirms at the thought of mashing these spirits together, which from a taste perspective I can certainly relate to. But if you are of the viewpoint that you are likely to become more drunk mixing these five base spirits than if you were to consume the equivalent volume of alcohol in a cocktail containing only one or two base spirits… I'm going to have to disappoint you. There's no proof that mixing drinks increases your level of drunkenness, or that it improves your chance of contracting a bad hangover. What does cause drunkenness is drinking lots of alcohol in a short time, which is a practice that tends to go hand in hand with cross-discipline imbibing… and Long Island Iced Teas.

# WILBURY SOUR

60 ML/2 FL. OZ. WILBURY SPIRIT (*see opposite*)
20 ML/⅔ FL. OZ. FRESH LEMON JUICE
10 ML/⅓ FL. OZ. SUGAR SYRUP (*see page 32*)
½ EGG WHITE • SODA WATER

Shake all of the ingredients once with cubed ice, then strain and shake again with no ice to create a foamy head. Pour into a small, chilled highball glass. Top up with a splash of soda water. **Note:** I've also tried this recipe with an egg yolk in place of the white (a golden fizz) and it works remarkably well!

Let's begin with this twist on a Long Island Iced Tea by getting one thing straight: half of the ingredients in a Long Island Iced Tea are totally pointless.

It's not that they don't serve a functional purpose (this is alcohol we're talking about, after all), but rather that they don't serve a *taste* purpose. Take vodka, for example. There's no way you're tasting vodka when it's smothered in tequila, citrus and Coke. Sure, you'll appreciate the alcohol it supplies, but using more tequila would have the same effect. Gin struggles for attention here too, as does rum if it's the unaged, Cuban-style rum that most bars opt for.

So that just leaves the triple sec, tequila, citrus and Coke (that's right, a Long Island is basically a cola-flavoured margarita, served long). And I grant you, it tastes OK, but that doesn't get away from the truth of the matter, which is that the Long Island Iced Tea is the product of sloppy mixology. That long list of disparate spirits dares you to order it because it sounds so ridiculous. It's a cute but slightly vicious mongrel living in a world of classic cocktails bred from pedigree spirits.

That's why there's a kind of unwritten rule in drinks' creation that you shouldn't mix two different base spirits in the same cocktail. By doing so, you tend to contaminate both liquids and sacrifice nuance. Flavours become indistinct and you lose the all-important sense of definition about the genetics of the drink. The Long Island Iced Tea as a prime example of this.

But rules (especially unwritten rules) are made to be broken, and it got me wondering whether it's possible to combine, say, four or five different base spirits and create some kind of a hybrid spirit that is genuinely better than the sum of its parts? The Traveling Wilburys of spirits, perhaps?

Strictly speaking, blending spirits is nothing new. Most spirits are blended in one way or another, whether it's a blending of casks from the same distillery, or a blend of spirits from more than one distillery, as with blended Scotch whisky. For this drink, however, I will be blending spirits from five unique regions made from four different base materials. The same principles apply, though: establish aromatic harmony between top, middle and bottom notes, and achieve a good mouthfeel and depth of flavour.

My starting point for this supergroup is Cognac. I'll use the other spirits to amplify various characteristics of the Cognac and the result will be a kind of mutant Cognac that tastes like no other. An aged *rhum agricole* will introduce tropical fruits, banana, and a slight vegetal characteristic; a single malt aged in sherry casks will offer bass notes of concentrated soft, dried fruit; citrus vodka will give lemony top notes; and absinthe will add anise and more vegetal depth in the mid-palate.

The spirit tastes superb on its own, but this is a twist on a Long Island Iced Tea, so I serve it as a straight-up fizz-style cocktail.

## WILBURY SPIRIT

200 ML/6¾ FL. OZ. VSOP COGNAC (*try* HENNESSY *or* FRAPIN)
125 ML/4¼ FL. OZ. SHERRY-CASK SINGLE MALT WHISKY (*try* GLENFARCLAS 15 *or* THE MACALLAN 12)
75 ML/2½ FL. OZ. AGED RHUM AGRICOLE (*try* RHUM JM *or* TROIS RIVIÈRES)
75 ML/2½ FL. OZ. CITRUS VODKA (*try* BELVEDERE CITRUS *or* KETEL ONE CITROEN)
25 ML/¾ FL. OZ. ABSINTHE (*try* LA CLANDESTINE *or* JADE 1901)

*Makes 500 ml/17 fl. oz.*

# GIN

# BREAKFAST MARTINI

50 ML/1⅔ FL. OZ. BEEFEATER 24 GIN • 15 ML/½ FL. OZ. COINTREAU
15 ML/½ FL. OZ. LEMON JUICE • 10 G/⅓ OZ. ORANGE MARMALADE

Add all the ingredients to a shaker and give them a good stir with a spoon to break up the
marmalade. Next add the ice, and shake well for 10 seconds. Double-strain into a chilled
Martini glass and garnish with a thin twist of orange zest.

If you ask me, there's nothing wrong with drinking a regular Dry Martini for breakfast, but I can certainly see why a double measure of slightly diluted gin and whisper of vermouth might not fit into everyone's morning routine (must be the olive garnish). Perhaps that's why, in 1996, Salvatore 'The Maestro' Calabrese developed a slightly more accessible companion to a bowl of cornflakes.

Salvatore was running the Library Bar at the Lanesborough Hotel in London at the time, and I guess there's no better place to serve a breakfast cocktail than in a posh hotel bar. The drink was well received, so when Salvatore went to New York the following year to promote the launch of his book *Classic Cocktails*, he convinced legendary bartender Dale DeGroff to let him serve it at New York's Rainbow Room bar. According to Salvatore, 'Dale thought [he] was mad using marmalade in a cocktail.'

The drink bears a good deal of resemblance to at least two classic Savoy drinks that also feature in this book. First is the Corpse Reviver No. 2 (see pages 114–5), where the similarly bracing tang of sweet and sour places the Breakfast Martini firmly in the pick-me-up category of mixed drinks for the morning after the night before. Second is the White Lady (see pages 118–9), the difference here being the lack of egg white (which most agree is essential to a White Lady) and the inclusion of marmalade, with a slight fiddle with the ratios to accommodate it.

But that's not the only Harry Craddock drink that this drink is related to. There's also the Marmalade Cocktail. Originally printed in Craddock's famous 1930

work *The Savoy Cocktail Book*, the Marmalade Cocktail was intended to serve six people. Craddock remarked: 'By its bitter-sweet taste this cocktail is especially suited to be a luncheon aperitif.' The drink called for '2 Dessertspoonful [sic] Orange Marmalade, The Juice of 1 big or 2 small Lemon, 4 Glasses Gin', to be shaken and garnished with a twist of orange.

Personally, I find the Marmalade Cocktail a little too tart. A glug of sugar syrup soon sorts the problem out, or the other option is a splash of triple sec. Of course, by that point you're drinking a Breakfast Martini.

Salvatore tells me that the inspiration for the cocktail didn't come from old drinks books, but from his wife. Being Italian, Salvatore is not in the habit of eating breakfast – a shot of espresso usually suffices. But working late nights takes its toll, and on one occasion when he emerged from bed looking particularly haggard, a slice of toast with marmalade was forcefully shoved into his mouth. 'The bittersweet tang reminded me of the sweet and sour balance of a good cocktail,' he says. The rest of the process came easily: gin for juniper freshness; triple sec to sweeten and to heighten the orange aromatics, and lemon to balance.

Some will argue that the Breakfast Martini is a simple twist on a White Lady, or a copy of the Marmalade. For me it's arbitrary whether Salvatore adapted the drink or came up with it entirely independently, because what we know for sure is that very few, if any, bartenders were making cocktails with marmalade in 1997. Salvatore changed that, inventing a tasty, innovative drink that used an ingredient common to every household, restaurant and – from then onwards – bar.

# CONTINENTAL MARTINI

20 ML/⅔ FL. OZ. COLD CEYLON TEA • 10 G/⅓ OZ. LINDEN HONEY
20 ML/⅔ FL. OZ. TURBO BERGAMOT JUICE (*see method below*)
50 ML/1⅔ FL. OZ. HEPPLE GIN • 15 G/½ OZ. EGG WHITE

Peel 5 bergamots using a potato peeler. Avoid the pith where possible. Weigh your peels and add them to a ziplock/sous vide bag along with the same weight in water. This should be enough to make 10 cocktails. Drop the bag into a water bath set to 60°C/140°F for 4 hours. While the peels are cooking, juice your bergamots and strain the liquid through muslin/cheesecloth. Once the peels have cooked for 4 hours, strain them out and reserve the liquid. Next, mix your bergamot juice with the peel infusion at a ratio of 3:1. This is your Turbo Bergamot Juice, and if you like you can freeze this juice in 20 ml/⅔ oz. ice cube moulds until needed.

To build the drink, add everything to a shaker (defrost the bergamot juice first) and shake well with cubed ice. Shake again without the ice and pour into a chilled Martini glass.

Shortly after Salvatore created his Breakfast Martini, another drink was being developed in New York City. The drink's creator was Audrey Saunders, who at the time was working at Bemelmans Bar at the Carlyle Hotel. Audrey's drink also had a breakfast theme about it and was based on gin and lemon juice, but instead of using marmalade it called for Earl Grey tea-infused gin. She named it the Earl Grey MarTEAni.

Also around that time, with some inspiration from the drinks mentioned above, I developed a cocktail that called for gin, Earl Grey tea, grapefruit juice and honey. I named it the Continental Martini because all of the ingredients (OK, perhaps not the gin) tend to feature in a Continental breakfast buffet. As it happens, all of the ingredients tend to pair quite well together too.

Honey and citrus are a no-brainer as a pairing, and honey is a fantastic alternative sweetener that works in a whole variety of drinks. Honey also pairs well with gin (see the Bee's Knees cocktail – another Audrey Saunders creation), elevating some of the earthy spice qualities with its sweetness and depth of finish. And then there's the tea.

Tea cocktails really don't get the attention they deserve, especially considering that tea was used widely in punches back in the 17th and 18th centuries, but few drinks these days capitalise on the flavour and complexity that tea can offer to a serve. My original recipe called for Earl Grey tea, which is flavoured with bergamot oil. This citrus oil comes from the zest of a small- to medium-sized yellow- or green-coloured orange. Only thing is, most Earl Grey tea is actually flavoured with ingredients that simulate the bright zestiness of the bergamot. Indeed, there probably aren't enough bergamots on the planet to flavour all of the Earl Grey tea that is consumed, and most of the natural oil ends up in cosmetics rather than tea bags (around one-third of all perfumes contain bergamot).

In the year 2000 pink grapefruit juice worked as a good substitute for bergamot, but when I finally encountered fresh bergamots in around 2010 the intensely perfumed character of the fruit won me over, so I swapped the grapefruit out (sorry grapefruit, I still love you). As a result, I also swapped the Earl Grey for good-quality Ceylon tea, as there are plenty of citrus characteristics in the latter.

The recipe above calls for fresh bergamots, which are a little easier to come by than they used to be, but are still the preserve of specialist fruit sellers. It's likely that your bergamots will come from southern Italy, and they tend to be available through the late autumn and early winter. Given their scarcity (and high price) it's essential that you get the most out of the fruit, so I've included strategies to preserve the valuable skin oils, and I suggest freezing any excess juice you might have.

The egg white is optional, but less optional than usual… if that makes sense. This is because the tannin in the tea can taste astringent and the proteins in egg white bind to the tannin, softening the flavour.

# HANKY-PANKY

40 ML / 1 ⅓ FL. OZ. PLYMOUTH GIN
40 ML / 1 ⅓ FL. OZ. MARTINI ROSSO
5 ML / 1 TEASPOON FERNET-BRANCA

Pour all of the ingredients into a mixing beaker and add plenty of ice cubes. Stir for at least a minute, then strain into a chilled Martini glass. Spritz a small disc of orange zest over the top.

I'm not sure there are many people still alive that throw the phrase 'hanky-panky' into their normal conversations. It has become an outdated and deeply uncool way of describing illicit sexual relations and tends only to be uttered by people too prudish to proffer further details of exactly what the relations entailed.

But if you were involved in hanky-panky prior to the 1950s, it's unlikely to have involved an act of a sexual nature. In the late 19th century, hanky-panky had a broader scope covering any act that was unethical or underhand.

When the term first came about, in the 1830s, it was specifically related to paranormal trickery and the belief in ghosts and apparitions. Perhaps the phrase came from the much older 'hocus-pocus'. After all, it does share the same initials, it rhymes, and has a similar definition. That may also be why 'hanky-panky' was widely adopted by magicians to describe illusions and sleight-of-hand trickery.

In 1912, *Hanky Panky* was the title of a short-lived musical that opened at the Broadway Theatre in New York. The fact that the phrase had moved into the lexicon of general entertainers is an important event, because it is a thespian that we have to thank for the naming of the Hanky-Panky cocktail.

This occurred around the same time as the stage musical, but specifics are difficult to come by. What we do know is that the drink was invented by Ada 'Coley' Coleman at the Savoy's American Bar in London. Coley worked at the Savoy from 1903 to 1924, during a period when women were not permitted to drink in there.

Coleman created the Hanky-Panky for actor Charles Hawtrey (1858–1923) who, when he wasn't starring in West End musicals and silent movies, spent a great deal of time gambling, drinking and getting married/divorced. Coleman told the story behind the creation of the Hanky-Panky to *The People* newspaper in 1925:

*The late Charles Hawtrey… was one of the best judges of cocktails that I knew. Some years ago, when he was overworking, he used to come into the bar and say, 'Coley, I am tired. Give me something with a bit of punch in it.' It was for him that I spent hours experimenting until I had invented a new cocktail. The next time he came in, I told him I had a new drink for him. He sipped it, and, draining the glass, he said, 'By Jove! That is the real hanky-panky!' And Hanky-Panky it has been called ever since.*

The drink consisted of equal parts dry gin and sweet vermouth accompanied by a splash of Fernet-Branca and a twist of orange. The fact that it called for the more modern dry gin over Old Tom and that it is essentially a sweet Martini with the addition of Fernet, suggests that it was conceived in the 1910s, after the trend for dry gin and dry vermouth in early Martini cocktails that appeared in the first decade of the 20th century. The drink shares a great deal of similarity to Gin & It (equal parts gin and Italian vermouth), which became very popular in London during Prohibition (1920–33). It seems likely then that the drink was created between 1910 and 1920. And since it's unlikely that Hawtrey was 'overworking' during World War I, I would place its creation at some point between 1910 and 1914.

# THE COLE HOLE

2 LITRES/QUARTS BOLS 'ORIGINAL' GENEVER
(*or any other unaged, high moutwijn-content genever*)
1.75 LITRES/QUARTS COCCHI ROSSO VERMOUTH
250 ML/8½ FL. OZ. FERNET-BRANCA
500 ML/17 FL. OZ. MINERAL WATER

*5-litre/5¼-quart barrel – makes approximately 35 drinks*

Step one is to acquire a 5-litre/quart barrel and season it. Casks used for spirits' maturation are normally seasoned with sherry or American whiskey. You can season your cask with whatever you like, but it's important to understand the purpose of seasoning, which is to draw out the initial hit of strong wood and vanilla characteristics. If you don't season your barrel, these flavours will quickly envelop your drink. In this instance, I recommend seasoning with a cheap red wine. Pour a bottle in (or two depending on the size of your barrel) and leave to sit for a week or so, rotating the barrel daily. After a week has passed, empty the cask, add 200 ml/6¾ fl. oz. of cold water that has been boiled and leave the bung off the barrel to prevent mould/mold.

Empty the barrel of any leftover water. Mix the ingredients together (scale the quantities if you are using a larger or smaller barrel) then pour into the barrel using a funnel. Seal the barrel and, for best results, store in sheltered outdoor location such as a shed or garage.

The time required in-barrel will vary depending on the activity of the cask as well as your own taste preferences. Taking regular cask samples is part of the pleasure of barrel ageing. If, when you decide to empty your barrel and bottle your cocktail, you decide it has too much wood character, simply blend some more of the unaged cocktail back in to the mature one.

Pour 130 ml/4½ fl. oz. of the cocktail over ice and strain into a chilled Martini glass. Garnish with a light spritz of orange oils.

It's ironic that most of the bars that experiment with barrel-aged cocktails tend to do so with cocktails that call for an aged base spirit. Whether it's a Manhattan containing bourbon or rye, or a Sazerac made with Cognac, bartenders are electing for expertly crafted products, then putting them back in a barrel (along with other ingredients) to… improve them? Perhaps it's the comfort of the knowledge that they are using a product that can withstand a little maturation character, but whatever it is, it's a mistake. Sure, I know bartenders who are masters at blending together flavours, but the art of nurturing a spirit through maturation in cask is pure sorcery that cannot be learned easily or quickly.

Far better then, to set your barrel-ageing sights at a cocktail that doesn't contain an aged-spirit component.

This way you're creating an entirely new, one-of-a-kind drink that has no rule book to follow or flavour profile to conform to.

The Hanky-Panky is a great contender for this kind of treatment. This is because it uses a white, unaged spirit as its base ingredient, but it also contains those powerful spice and eucalyptus flavours that come from the vermouth and the Fernet-Branca, which will be enthusiastically welcomed when the drink does battle with the barrel.

To make this drink you will of course need to buy a barrel. I recommend purchasing a barrel of at least 5 litres/5¼ quarts, but the bigger the better (the limiting factor in this will probably be how much alcohol you are prepared to buy to fill it). A 5-litre/

5¼-quart barrel can be bought for as little as £26/$37 (a 20-litre/21-quart barrel is about twice that) and tend to be sourced from one of the growing numbers of cooperages in eastern Europe. Be sure to follow my guidelines for buying and filling barrels on page 53.

Now, while I'm confident that Fernet-Branca and vermouth can withstand the effects of oak, the gin is another story. There are a growing number of barrel-aged gins on the market nowadays, but very few of them get it right in my experience. Delicate botanicals struggle to shine through once a cask has its wicked way and the liquids tend to take on a green, sappy kind of character that is overlaid (rather than combined) with brash vanilla and coconut. But there is a type of gin (of sorts) that is not just capable of being barrel-aged, but performs very well when put in a cask: genever. Genever comes in both aged and unaged styles, but all of my favourite genevers contain a high *moutwijn* content, meaning there is more of the characterful, malt spirit in their recipe. These styles can not only take a hit of cask character on the chin, but they pull it into a loving embrace.

I've named this drink the Cole Hole, after both Ada Coleman and the Coal Hole pub next door to the Savoy in London, which was formerly the coal storage cellar for the hotel. A barrel is a coal hole of a different type – a wooden sanctuary for drinks, lined with that thin layer of charcoal – and the ink-black appearance of this drink will certainly have you believing it is born from coal (or a Coleman).

# TOM COLLINS

50 ML/1⅔ FL. OZ. OLD TOM GIN • 25 ML/¾ FL. OZ. STRAINED LEMON JUICE
10 ML/⅓ FL. OZ SUGAR SYRUP (*see page 32*) • SODA WATER

Add the gin, lemon juice and sugar to a highball glass filled with plenty of ice.
Gently stir while slowly topping up with soda. Add more ice as required.
Garnish with a slice of orange.

It's no secret that many of the best-known drinks out there have their origins in punches. The term 'punch' comes from the Hindi word for five (*panch*) and is thought to represent the five styles of ingredient that are essential to all punches: strong, long, sour, sweet and spice. It's a formula that is applicable to so many mixed drinks that it's a wonder punches aren't better recognised for what they are: cocktails in the embryonic stage of evolution.

Take the Tom Collins, for example. It's a drink that became very popular in late-19th century America, but it's actually based on an old English punch recipe. The history of the Tom Collins takes us back to some of the earliest gin punches, which featured on menus in some of Mayfair's legendary nicotine-stained gentlemen's clubs, like Limmer's Hotel and the Garrick Club.

In 1830, the bar manager of the Garrick Club was an American man called Stephen Price. He was an early advocate of iced soda water, which, when paired with gin, would have then seemed a strange combination. As David Wondrich notes in *Punch* (2011), 'soda water [was] a popular hangover cure... seen as an antidote to punch, not an accomplice'. The Garrick Club Punch recipe was published in *The London Quarterly* in 1835 and included 'half a pint of gin, lemon peel, lemon juice, sugar, maraschino, a pint and a quarter of water, and two bottles of iced soda water'. It became an international sensation.

Meanwhile, the bar at Limmer's Hotel on Conduit Street was being managed by a plump yet dignified head waiter by the name of John Collins. Collins had a handful of punch recipes up his tailored sleeves, but the most enduring of these – and the one that would later carry his name through every cocktail bar on the planet – was known simply as Limmer's Punch. The recipe was much the same as the Garrick Club drink, but instead of maraschino it used *capillaire*, a kind of sugar syrup that is aromatised with orange flower water.

Collins' drink also became recognised for its fizz, as well as its near-perfect balance of sweet, sour and aromatic elements. It was, and remains today, one of the best mixed drinks on the planet. As American cocktail culture took off through the mid-1800s, it was the reliable large-format serves, like Limmer's Punch, that got the single-serve treatment. And what better name for this sweet and sour fizzy delight than the name of its creator: John Collins.

A John Collins called for the most popular gin in America at the time, which was Holland's Gin (aka genever), but when the new, lighter style of London gin called Old Tom found its way to American shores (and genever fell out of fashion), John was changed to Tom and a new classic was made.

Unlike a Gin Fizz, which shares the same ingredients, a Tom Collins is built straight into a glass and simply stirred before serving (like a punch). It's also served with plenty of cubed ice, whereas a proper Gin Fizz should be served straight up. The absence of ice in the Fizz means there's nothing to get in the way of wolfing the whole thing back in one satisfying gulp. A Collins demands you take a bit more time. As the contents of the glass recedes and the drink is gently stirred, the ice cubes eventually lose the ability to balance on one another, so they fall, clinking as they go like the most discreet alarm in the world, reminding you that it might be time to... order another?

# LACTOM COLLINS

································································

25 ML/¾ FL. OZ. TANQUERAY LONDON DRY GIN
5 ML/1 TEASPOON LEMON JUICE • 10 ML/⅓ FL. OZ. LUXARDO MARASCHINO LIQUEUR
50 ML/1⅔ FL. OZ. GOSE BEER (*also consider* LAMBIC *and* BERLINER WEISSE)
50 ML/1⅔ FL. OZ. SODA WATER

Take a chilled highball, fill it with cubed ice and the gin, lemon and maraschino. Stir well, then top up with beer and soda. Give it another quick stir. I like to garnish this drink with a thin slice of hard goats' cheese. Goats' cheese is relatively high in acid, and pairing it with this drink brings out fruit qualities in the cheese and spice notes in the cocktail.

Naturally, the brand of beer and brand of gin that you use to make this cocktail will steer the final flavour of the drink. I've listed two specific types, but I would encourage you to use what is available and experiment with matching the gin botanicals with the character of the sour beer.

There are few drinks that can compete with the pre-dinner might of a Tom Collins. It's everything you want from an aperitif: long, effervescent, slightly sour and easy to quaff down quickly if your food arrives faster than you expected it to. In fact, there are only a handful of drinks that can compete with a Tom Collins in this discipline, but one of them is an ice-cold glass of beer. And as the old saying goes, 'if you can't beat them, join them' and that's exactly what I intend to do.

Beer cocktails are difficult to get right, though, and have a tendency to end up tasting like the contents of a drip tray in a busy nightclub. The trick is to use the beer sparingly, or to find a beer that is sufficiently stylised (coffee stout, raspberry kriek, etc.) to stand up well to mixing. For this drink, I'm using a style of beer that sits closer to the Tom Collins than any other: sour.

Sour beers are brewed, like any other beer, by the action of yeast with fermentable sugars that are extracted from cooked cereals. Where sours deviate from the norm is through the intentional addition of wild yeast and/or bacteria. The yeast strain *Brettanomyces* (aka *Brett*) is commonly employed to help with this process because, unlike regular brewer's yeast (*Saccharomyces cerevisiae*), it produces funky flavours reminiscent of citrus fruit, wine, hay barn, musk and butter. It gives the beer a ripe funk that you tend to love or hate. The actual sourness of a sour beer comes from the addition of the bacteria

*Lactobacillus*. Like yeast, it ferments sugar into alcohol and $CO_2$, but it also produces acetic and lactic acid – the cause of the vinegary, sour flavour that gives sour beer its tart, refreshing quality. The result is a beer that is delicious to drink from the bottle and better suited as a cocktail ingredient than regular ales and lagers.

My recipe attempts to highlight bright, citrus spices present in some gins, and fuse them with the acidity of the beer, opening up both aromatic and taste vibrancy. I also want to wrangle with the fruitiness of the drink which, for a drink containing sour beer, is a little trickier than you might think.

Fruits tend to get their natural sourness from citric and malic acids and, to a lesser extent, tartaric, ascorbic and succinic acids. Lactic and acetic acids (which dominate the flavour of sour beer) barely feature, which explains why sour beers can taste 'sour' but not exactly 'fruity'. But when all is said and done, this is a Collins cocktail, so I'm including lemon juice in my recipe, which will contribute a more conventional fruity tang.

To counteract all this acidity it will be necessary to sweeten slightly. This could be achieved with regular sugar syrup, but I'm opting for maraschino liqueur. The sweet-cherry flavour will come alive when hit with the range of acids present in the drink, and the net result will be a zingy spiced-citrus and cherry Collins, reminiscent of the tart candies I sucked on as a child.

································································

# CORPSE REVIVER NO. 2

20 ML/⅔ FL. OZ. PLYMOUTH GIN
20 ML/⅔ FL. OZ. TRIPLE SEC
20 ML/⅔ FL. OZ. LILLET BLANC
20 ML/⅔ FL. OZ. LEMON JUICE
2 DASHES ABSINTHE VERT

Add all of the ingredients to a cocktail shaker along with plenty of cubed ice. Shake well, then fine-strain into a chilled cocktail glass. You may like to garnish with a strip of lemon, but it's not essential, since the drink will all be gone in under a minute. Won't it?

There is something undeniably special about a recipe that calls for equal measures of every ingredient. These are the kind of cocktails that – despite being mixtures of disparate ingredients, some distilled, some fermented, and some fresh – have a certain inevitability that can only be of divine origin. Negroni, Last Word (see pages 122–3) and Gimlet are all great examples of equal-measure drinks. Another example is the Corpse Reviver No. 2 – or it would be were it not for the drink's most important ingredient: absinthe.

Corpse Revivers were once a whole family of cocktails, dispensed as hangover cures in the morning and as pick-me-ups in the afternoon and early evening. At the beginning of the 20th century it was common for a bar to offer their own proprietary formula for bringing pre-noon patrons back from the brink of death, and these were often listed as Corpse Revivers. Very few of these recipes were ever written down, though, perhaps on account of the questionable effectiveness of the promised revival or the sheer bizarreness of the concoctions, until Harry Craddock listed two in *The Savoy Cocktail Book* in 1930.

But a little digging around tells us that hangover cures have been called Corpse Revivers since at least the early 1860s, some 15 years before Harry Craddock was born. One of the earliest examples I could find features in an 1862 short story entitled *How I Stopped The Brownes From Asking Me To Come To Dinner*, where the narrator visits an American Bar (no, not that one)

in London's Piccadilly and is served a Corpse Reviver containing milk and some other unnamed alcoholic ingredients. The drink was thrown between two crystal vessels and, upon drinking it, the narrator remarked that it 'filled [him] with an extraordinary courage and determination'.

Of the two revivers that Craddock penned in *The Savoy Cocktail Book*, the Corpse Reviver No. 2 is the best known and, to be frank, the best (No. 1 was featured in my first book and is a very different, brandy-based drink). The No. 2 combines gin with triple sec and lemon juice, so were it not for the addition of Lillet Blanc and the aforementioned slug of absinthe, it would effectively be a White Lady (see pages 118–9). But those two simple modifiers transform the cocktail into something else entirely – the Lillet smoothes over some of the craggy edges of the lemon and orange liqueur, while the absinthe brings herbal zing and adds a kind of ghostly glaucous to the drink's hue.

Craddock commented that 'Four of these taken in swift succession will un-revive the corpse again.' His point being that overdosing on the drink would result in the drinker once again inducing a death-like state.

When four out the five ingredients in your cocktail are alcoholic and three of them are strong spirits, it's wise to approach with caution. With that in mind, I like to make small Corpse Revivers… dainty little things that can be knocked back in a couple of sips like the medicine that they are intended to be.

# FIRST AID KIT

25 ML/¾ FL. OZ. SEEDLIP GARDEN 108
35 ML/1¼ FL. OZ. TONIC WATER
20 ML/⅔ FL. OZ. SWEET FENNEL & THYME TEA (*see opposite*)
15 ML/½ FL. OZ. FRESH LEMON JUICE

Mix all of the ingredients together and package in a 100 ml/3½ fl. oz. plastic pouch. Screw the cap on loosely and place in the freezer until required. Grab one from the freezer on your way out and enjoy chilled once fully defrosted (alternatively, this is a delicious non-alcoholic cocktail to enjoy on any occasion).

If you remember back to my first book, *The Curious Bartender: The Artistry and Alchemy of Creating the Perfect Cocktail*, you might recall my creative twist on the Corpse Reviver No. 1, which involved pre-batching the drink in a glass bottle that could be stored in the fridge and opened quickly in times of desperate need (basically, during the course of any normal hangover). I thought this a fun approach to the Corpse Reviver cocktail, since mixing cocktails is nobody's idea of a fun morning after. So it's with that in mind that I plan to continue this theme of instant revival with my twist on the Corpse Reviver No.2.

The only problem with this strategy is that it relies on your ability to get home in the first instance, and it then requires you to be capable of getting to (and opening) the fridge the next morning. Neither are a given. The need for liquid therapy is.

The only solution then is to carry the cocktail with you. Pop it in your bag or jacket pocket and then forget about it until you wake up on your mate's living-room floor with all your money missing and a stray dog licking your face.

A hip flask will do the trick, but my experience of hip flasks is that they get drunk and misplaced with surprising ease. The solution is some kind of expendable hip flask, but since no such thing exists, the next best thing is a foil Capri-Sun-style pouch. Now, I actually have a fair bit of experience with these kinds of containers because a sideline business I run called WHISKY-ME delivers monthly drams of whisky through letterboxes in flexible plastic pouches. Plastic and foil spout pouches are extremely cheap, almost indestructible and reusable many times over (so needn't be bad for the environment). They're also happy to be frozen, which will prove beneficial for my Corpse Reviver twist.

For the drink itself, I'm going to attempt one of the most ambitious cocktail remodelling exercises that I have ever undertaken… by making it *non-alcoholic*.

That's right, this will be a purely non-alcoholic interpretation of a Corpse Reviver because, let's face it, no matter how good it might feel at the time, the last thing your body needs during the hangover from hell is more alcohol. My non-alco interpretation of this classic substitutes gin for a brand of distilled botanical 'spirit' called Seedlip, effectively switching triple sec for orange-peel oils. Then, through a combination of tonic water, fresh thyme and fennel tea, I can create a flavour that's not dissimilar to that of absinthe mixed with vermouth.

This is one of those drinks that tastes like it'll do you good. And that's because, for once, it really will!

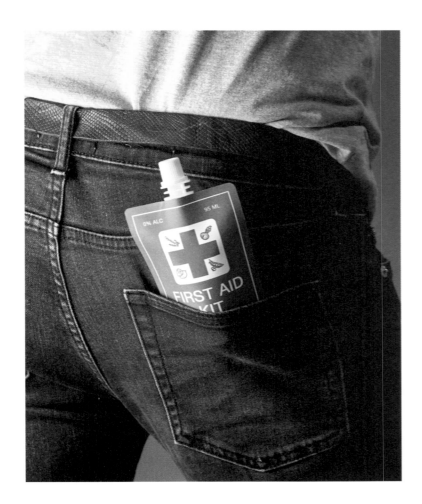

## SWEET FENNEL & THYME TEA

150 ML/5 FL. OZ. BOILING WATER
1 FENNEL TEA BAG
1 SPRIG FRESH THYME
50 G/1¾ OZ. SUGAR
1 G/4 PINCHES SALT

Brew all of the ingredients together in a jug/pitcher and strain.
Refrigerate for up to a week until required.

# WHITE LADY

50 ML/1⅔ FL. OZ. GIN
15 ML/½ FL. OZ. COINTREAU
10 ML/⅓ FL. OZ. LEMON JUICE
10 G/⅓ OZ. EGG WHITE

Add all of the ingredients to a cocktail shaker and shake with cubed ice.
Double-strain into a chilled coupe glass. No garnish necessary.

The White Lady belongs to that same family of cocktails as the Margarita, Sidecar and Cosmopolitan in that it's a modified sour, or as is the case, sweetened, by the inclusion of either triple sec or orange Curaçao (more on this shortly). This tradition of liqueur-ising classic sours dates back as far as the Brandy Crusta, a drink that was invented in New Orleans in the 1840s, and for reasons that I documented in *The Curious Bartender: The Artistry and Alchemy of Creating the Perfect Cocktail*, is the Ford Model T of cocktails.

There's just one slight problem with the New Orleans sour family of drinks, and that is they usually don't taste very good. Most often this is a fault of the bartender, who tends to refer to early-20th-century specifications of these drinks that call for too much citrus and too much liqueur modifier. The effect is something saccharine, flabby and altogether disagreeable, to the point where you find yourself taking great gulps of the cocktail so that the whole sorry business may be put to bed as quickly as possible. On the other hand, if you dial back the modifying ingredients slightly and allow the base spirit to shine, you can end up with a tasty, refreshing drink that's perfect as a pre-dinner sharpener.

The first documented recipe for the White Lady was published in Harry Craddock's *The Savoy Cocktail Book* (1930), and it's for that reason that the drink has an enduring association with the American Bar at the Savoy. But the American Bar is the most famous bar in cocktail history that didn't actually invent many classic cocktails (the trail runs dry after Hanky-Panky [see pages 106–7] and Corpse Reviver No. 2 [see pages 114–5], and the White Lady was not born there either.

It was instead invented by one other famous Harry of the mixologists' stable – Harry MacElhone.

The son of a jute-mill owner from Dundee, Scotland, MacElhone began bartending at the age of 21, in 1911, at No. 5 Rue Daunou in Paris. Twelve years later, having worked through bars in New York and London, he would buy that bar and rename it Harry's New York Bar, which is today better known as simply Harry's Ba. It was while working at Ciro's Club in London that Harry first created a drink called White Lady.

Originally comprising two parts Cointreau to one part crème de menthe and one part lemon juice, the drink tasted like a bad throat lozenge and looked like that suspicious kind of swimming-pool water. It's a wonder he didn't lose his job. By the time he opened Harry's Bar in Paris, he had seen sense, removing the crème de menthe, knocking back the Cointreau and adding a healthy slug of gin. He also added some egg white, which besides giving the drink a foamy head, also produced a cool, white opacity that was like the visual equivalent of a snowball hitting you in the teeth.

This newly formulated White Lady, as with the White Lady recipe printed in *The Savoy Cocktail Book*, called for two parts gin to one part each of Cointreau and lemon juice. Craddock's recipe omitted the egg white. If you try a White Lady like this, you might find it's prone to all that flabby, saccharine regret – there's a whole shot of Cointreau in there, for goodness' sake! I suggest dialling them down a little and allowing the gin to do its thing. When you get it right, this is a wonderful drink, and the undisputed queen of the New Orleans sour family (for what it is).

# PURE BRILLIANT WHITE LADY

## WHITE TEA GIN

### 700 ML/24 FL. OZ. GIN • 30 G/1 OZ. WHITE TEA

There are a few different ways of making this, the easiest one being a simple, cold maceration in a bottle over the course of a week. The quicker route is a sous-vide infusion at 70°C/158°F for approximately an hour. The *best* method and the most efficient use of your expensive white tea leaves is to use liquid nitrogen. Put the tea leaves in a double-walled steel bowl or other insulated container. Pour enough liquid nitrogen over the leaves to cover them, then bash them into a fine powder using a rolling pin or muddler. Top up with more liquid nitrogen if the mixture dries out and begins to warm. Once the leaves are fully powdered, allow the nitrogen to evaporate off, then douse the leaves with gin. Mix thoroughly, then double-strain the gin through a chinois (conical sieve/strainer) and a paper filter to remove the tea.

## PURE BRILLIANT WHITE LADY

### 2 G/1/16 OZ. LECITHIN • 1 G/4 PINCHES SALT
### 25 G/1 OZ. MELTED COCONUT OIL • 650 ML/22 FL. OZ. WHITE TEA GIN (*see above*)
### 200 ML/6¾ FL. OZ. CLARIFIED LEMON JUICE (*see pages 46–8*)
### 100 ML/3½ FL. OZ. VANILLA GOMME SYRUP (*see page 205*)

Using an Aerolatte (milk frother) or a small whisk, blend the lecithin and salt into the coconut oil. Mix the gin, lemon juice and vanilla gomme together. Put the lecithin/coconut mixture in a blender or food processor and set to a medium speed, then slowly begin pouring in the gin mixture. The mixture should turn opaque as it forms an emulsion. Continue blending until the gin mixture is fully incorporated.

Pour the cocktail into a 1-litre/quart bottle and pop it into the freezer until needed.

To serve, shake the bottle well and then pour into a chilled Martini glass.

While it's possible to tweak the White Lady into something with above-average levels of quaffability, there was a niggling itch with this drink that I found difficult to scratch. It took me years to identify the source of my discomfort, but now that I have, I feel liberated as I also have the power to correct it. The problem, you see, is simple: the name is wrong. Well, it's not so much that the name is wrong, but that the drink doesn't quite fit the name. Don't get me wrong – White Lady is a fantastic name for a drink. It speaks of purity, elegance and discreetness. But the White Lady is a potent, sweet-and-sour lump of a drink, dressed in a coupe glass like a boxer in stilettos. It's white, but it's no lady.

I thought about simply changing the name of the drink, but that didn't present much of a challenge (Anglaisour would get my vote). So that left only one alternative, which was to change the ingredients.

The goal, then, was a simple one: create a new formula for the White Lady that drew upon all the themes that you might associate with the words 'white' and 'lady', but kept the spirit of the original cocktail alive.

To create a strong opaque whiteness, I dropped the egg white and instead opted to make a fat-and-water/alcohol emulsion. Preparing this is a bit like the process for making mayonnaise, only the proportions and the ingredients are different, it'll have a more

watery texture, and it'll taste different (so not much like a mayonnaise at all, really).

I use coconut oil as the base for this, for its clean, white-chocolate flavour and slightly grassy qualities. The melted oil is emulsified into the other ingredients using lecithin from soya beans/soybeans, which is a type of amphiphilic fat that attracts both water and oil, binding them together and preventing them from splitting apart (an emulsion).

The lighter, floral side of the coconut oil is elevated by the inclusion of homemade vanilla gomme syrup, and the grassy side is drawn out by the immaculately clean flavour of white tea infused into gin. A small amount of clarified lemon juice is used to add both balance and freshness.

My Pure Brilliant White Lady is as white as white emulsion paint, has all the clean, floral aromatics of linen drying on the washing line, and tastes like the breast milk of the gods. It is both the whitest-looking and whitest-tasting cocktail on the planet.

To drill this concept home completely, I serve the cocktail on a black backdrop. But not just any black backdrop! BLACK 2.0 is the most pigmented, flattest, mattest, black acrylic paint on the planet. Like a black hole, it absorbs 98 per cent of visible light, making my Pure Brilliant White Lady pop like a supernova.

# LAST WORD

25 ML/¾ FL. OZ. GREEN CHARTREUSE
25 ML/¾ FL. OZ. MARASCHINO LIQUEUR
25 ML/¾ FL. OZ. BEEFEATER GIN
25 ML/¾ FL. OZ. LIME JUICE
25 ML/¾ FL. OZ. WATER

Add all of the ingredients to a cocktail shaker filled with ice. Shake for 10 seconds
then double-strain the contents into a chilled Martini glass.

These days, terms like 'Prohibition-era cocktail' and 'forgotten classic' get thrown around a lot by bartenders. Both labels are ridiculous, since cocktails were prohibited during Prohibition and because a truly forgotten classic would, by definition, still be forgotten (not documented in detail in a cocktail book like this!). But if there were a drink that qualified for both titles, it would have to be the Last Word.

The Last Word was first documented in Ted Saucier's saucily titled *Bottoms Up*, published in 1951. In the book – which features around a dozen suggestive illustrations of ladies posing with drinks – Saucier attributes the cocktail to the Detroit Athletic Club, adding that '[the] cocktail was introduced around here about thirty years ago by Frank Fogarty'. This timeline places the drink's creation during the early years of Prohibition (1920–33), which is quite something, since this cocktail would have required not one, not two, but three quite specific bottles of booze during a time when even moonshine was difficult to come by.

It turns out that the cocktail was actually invented around five years before Prohibition started, as it appeared on the Athletic Club's 1916 menu, a year after the place opened. The cocktail was listed at 35¢, making it the most expensive drink on the menu, probably on account of the Chartreuse.

Apparently it was a popular drink, which is surprising because it reads like a drunken teenage punchbowl on paper: two powerfully flavoured liqueurs, plus gin and lime. But, amazingly, it works a treat. Naturally, it's the Green Chartreuse that plays the leading role, delivering herbal and floral qualities in waves. The maraschino provides an alternate form of sweetness, with a touch of fruit and a little spice, while the gin hops and squeaks away somewhere underneath all that liqueur. Then there's the lime. Never before has citrus been so essential in a drink. Here, the lime cuts through the significant sweetness of the liqueurs, softens the alcohol and provides brightness where none existed before.

As an equal-part combination of five unrelated liquids, Last Word is the work of genius. Assuming you like Chartreuse, that is (otherwise you have no hope).

If anything, the Chartreuse is the one ingredient of this drink that could and probably should be dialled down a touch. Its dominance is almost absolute, sometimes making it difficult to detect the maraschino and the gin at all, plus its impressive ABV (55 per cent) moves the drink from the 'approach with caution' category of cocktail straight into 'WARNING!'. Adding a splash of water to the shaker helps dilute some of the concentrated character of the drink, and I'd recommend it, since you're going to need all the water you can get after a few of these.

# LONG WORD

35 ML/1¼ FL. OZ. CHARTREUSE
35 ML/1¼ FL. OZ. MARASCHINO
35 ML/1¼ FL. OZ. MANZANILLA SHERRY
35 ML/1¼ FL. OZ. CLARIFIED LIME JUICE (*see pages 46–8*)
20 ML/⅔ FL. OZ. GOMME SYRUP
190 ML/6½ FL. OZ. MINERAL WATER
2 DROPS SALINE SOLUTION

*Makes 2*

Mix all of the ingredients together in a SodaStream bottle and chill in the freezer until close to freezing. Screw the bottle into the SodaStream machine and charge with gas until the pressure-release valve begins to vent. Slowly vent the gas from the bottle, being ready to retighten if the liquid foams. Charge again, stopping once the gas vents. Release the gas again, carefully. Charge one last time, unscrew the bottle and fix a cap on top. Chill until needed and pour into flute glasses. No garnish required.

As we've already discussed, the Last Word is a drink that could benefit from a little extra dilution. Indeed, any drink where 50 per cent of the ingredients are liqueurs and 75 per cent of the ingredients are alcoholic should consider dilution a sensible option. When a drink has a lot of strong flavours packed into a tight package, the relationship between those flavours can become fraught and it'll be your palate that suffers as a consequence. A Last Word cocktail is a marvel for the first few sips, but by the bottom of the glass you're ready for a beer.

Fortunately for us, this is not a difficult drink to lengthen out. All that's required is some water and a slight tweak of the sweet/sour balance. I'm replacing the Last Word's gin (yes, I am aware that this is the gin section) with manzanilla sherry and a splash of saline solution. I've found that these two ingredients add an amazing sea breeze/maritime note to the drink that highlights more savoury, almost seaweed notes, in the chartreuse. The maraschino gives that sweet-shop/candy store cherry flavour, which is balanced by the lime. The overall effect I'm going for here is akin to a boozy herbal lemonade, the perfect aperitif or just a nice long sipping drink that won't fatigue your palate.

I've designed this cocktail to be carbonated in a SodaStream (see pages 56–8) and then left in the fridge (or on ice) until you're ready to serve it. Treat it like a bottle of Champagne. I've used clarified lime juice in my recipe as I think the lime oil brings something great to this cocktail. You can, if you wish, use an acid blend, but whatever you do, you must make sure your liquid is totally clear before carbonating. If carbonation is all a little too much for you, you will get a similar drink, albeit less fizzy, by replacing the mineral water with soda water.

# BRONX

45 ML/1½ FL. OZ. GORDON'S GIN • 10 ML/⅓ FL. OZ. MARTINI ROSSO
10 ML/⅓ FL. OZ. MARTINI EXTRA DRY
25 ML/¾ FL. OZ. FILTERED ORANGE JUICE

Shake all of the ingredients with cubed ice and strain into a chilled coupe glass. This drink is perhaps improved by the use of blood orange juice, or through a combination of grapefruit juice and orange juice. Garnish with a fresh cherry.

**An interesting side note:** Bill Wilson (aka Bill W.), the founder of Alcoholics Anonymous, was once quoted saying that the first drink he could remember was a Bronx, which was given to him at a party during World War I.

Ask a group of bartenders to tell you what the ultimate classic cocktail is, and they will debate long and hard, suggesting such drinks as the Martini, Manhattan, Negroni and Daiquiri. Ask them to tell you which is the worst classic cocktail and they'll come to a decision pretty quickly: the Bronx.

Gin and vermouth is a holy union of ingredients. In virtually any ratio you can imagine, it just works. But throw a measure of orange juice into the mix and suddenly nothing works any more and everything tastes wrong. So why am I including the Bronx in this book? Well, everybody likes an underdog and I like the challenge of attempting to work out what went wrong with this once-popular cocktail and whether there's any way to salvage something delicious from the wreckage.

Like the Bobby Burns, this drink was the product of the long-since-demolished Waldorf-Astoria Hotel on Manhattan Island. It was first mixed in the hotel's Empire Room (the main restaurant) sometime around the turn of the 20th century by bartender Johnnie Solon. This Spanish-American war veteran claimed not to have named the drink after the New York borough, but after the newly opened Bronx Zoo.

When requested by a lunchtime guest to make something 'new', Solon used the Duplex cocktail (equal parts dry and sweet vermouth with orange bitters) as a starting point. Two jiggers of Gordon's gin and a jigger of orange juice were combined with a Duplex. Stars then shot across the noonday sky and African elephants bowed their heads in respect: a new cocktail was born.

As the waiter transported the yellow drink away from the bar, he turned and asked Solon what its name was. Solon remembered that patrons of the Waldorf-Astoria sometimes claimed they saw 'strange animals' after quite a few mixed drinks, which reminded him of his visit to the zoo just two days previously – 'Oh, you can tell him it's a Bronx,' he replied.

Make no mistake about it, this drink was a real hit at the time, especially on warmer days and where a spot of daytime refreshment was in order. And since New York boroughs were obviously a safe naming strategy for cocktails – the Bronx had joined the very popular Manhattan – it likely inspired the creation of the Brooklyn cocktail, too.

As I said earlier, the drink has fallen out of fashion of late. I feel that the contempt directed at the Bronx is not through the fault of the drink, but through a miscommunication of its purpose. At the time of its creation, this cocktail was an antidote to more boozy drinks like the Martini and Manhattan. The Bronx served as a crossover between sours and straight-up spirit-and-vermouth aperitifs. It offers botanical depth, winey top notes and a bite of a fruity acidity to keep you fresh. As a mid-afternoon alternative to Pimm's and lemonade, or a wine spritzer, the Bronx has the potential to shine (and it's in those situations that I suggest you mix one).

# GIRAFFE

## OJ ICE

1 LITRE/34 FL. OZ. FILTERED FRESH ORANGE JUICE • 2 G/¹⁄₁₆ OZ. AGAR
600 ML/20 FL. OZ. WATER • 100 G/3½ OZ. CASTER SUGAR
ORANGE FOOD COLOURING

To clarify the orange juice, follow the instructions for gel clarification on page 46. After filtering the gel, you should be left with around 600 ml/21 fl. oz. of clarified orange juice. Gently heat the water with the caster sugar, allow it to cool, then mix with your clarified orange. Add food colouring to boost the orange colour (personally I like to use quite a lot, so that the drink has a striking contrast). Cast your juice into long, column-style ice-cube moulds and pop them in the freezer until required.

## GIRAFFE

25 ML/¾ FL. OZ. GIN • 50 ML/1⅔ FL. OZ. GANCIA BIANCO
3 GOOD DASHES OF ORANGE BITTERS • 3–4 DASHES OJ ICE (see above)
SODA WATER

Stir the gin, vermouth and bitters over cubed ice and strain into a chilled highball glass.
Drop in your OJ Ice, then top up with soda.

In spite of my claims of the 'right time' and 'right place' for a Bronx, nobody I know seems to be satisfied with this drink. You might find a great bartender who can do the drink justice, but a bartender who is simply 'good' will tweak the recipe to eke out the orange juice, giving the cocktail more a boozy hit and shifting it ever closer to a Martinez – which is silly, because they might as well have just make a Martinez. The point that I think most of us are missing is that a Bronx is not a substitute for a Martini-style drink, but a substitute for a sour or fizz.

So I am serving my twist on a Bronx in a highball glass. But I think there's more to it than just the length and delivery of this drink, and to make sure there's nothing awry with the genetics of the ingredients, I ran some taste tests. Separating the drink back into its constituent parts, I mixed each ingredient equally with each of the other ingredients to see which pairings

worked and which didn't. This was what I found:
• Gin mixes well with both types of vermouth but tastes bad with just orange juice.
• Sweet vermouth mixes well with all the other ingredients, especially the gin.
• Dry vermouth mixes well with everything, especially the orange juice.
• Orange juice mixes well with the sweet vermouth and the dry vermouth, but not the gin.

When I crunched all that data, I realised the best type of Bronx would be one that goes light on the gin, heavy on the vermouth and light again on the orange juice. The main issue I encountered with the orange juice was not the flavour of orange, but rather the acidity of the juice, which didn't play nicely with gin. It occurred to me that a large slice of orange as a garnish would probably serve this drink better than using actual orange juice.

That would be a rather defeatist way of revolutionising a Bronx cocktail though, so I began to think of alternative strategies for getting orange into the drink. Bitters were the obvious next step, since there are plenty of orange bitters to choose from, and introducing orange bitters to vermouth and gin is a like dousing a portion of fish and chips with vinegar (it works). But with the orange juice plainly removed from the drink entirely, I needed to find away to introduce it back in – but in a measured way.

The solution was obvious: ice. Orange-juice ice is easy to make, but the texture is a bit mushy (think of an orange popsicle/ice pop) and ruins the appearance of the drink as it melts. So I experimented with clarifying the orange juice before freezing it. This worked better, presumably because it removed some of the pectin and other insoluble components out of the juice and caused it to freeze in a more uniform way. When mixing a long

Bronx with this ice, I found that it worked well, but the orange still brought about an unwelcome acidity. To counteract this, I diluted the orange juice down slightly, boosted the sugar to elevate those fresh orange esters, then added some colouring to make the ice cube look like it's packed full of flavour.

For the finished serve, I lost the sweet vermouth altogether, instead using Gancia Bianco, which is just about the sweetest 'dry' vermouth you can get. It basically performs the same role as sweet vermouth and dry vermouth mixed together would have done. When the gin, vermouth and bitters are mixed, the drink is almost water-white, which gives a sense of purity and freshness to the cocktail. When the orange ice is dropped in, the pre-chilling of the liquid ingredients means that the orange ice melts nice and slowly, gradually building up the orange flavour of the cocktail as you drink.

# ❧ RUM ❧

# CORN 'N' OIL

50 ML/1⅔ FL. OZ. AGED BARBADOS RUM
10 ML/⅓ FL. OZ. FRESH LIME JUICE
10 ML/⅓ FL. OZ. JOHN D. TAYLOR'S VELVET FALERNUM
FEW DASHES ANGOSTURA BITTERS

Shake everything except the bitters with cubed ice and strain into an ice-filled tumbler. Put a few dashes of Angostura bitters on top and garnish with a lime wedge.

Here is a drink with a title that seems to speak of nature, and of simpler times – an honest day's toil on the farm perhaps? It reminds us that the 'a' and 'd' in 'and' are expendable after all, but more importantly it shows us that a cocktail's name can indeed be formed from ingredients that don't feature in the recipe for the drink. There is no corn, or even corn-based spirit, in a Corn 'n' Oil. No oil, either.

Corn 'n' Oil is really just a rum sour that's spiked with the sweet and limey spiced liqueur called falernum. The earliest reference to falernum that I could find comes from the literary magazine *All the Year Round*, which was owned and edited by Charles Dickens, Jr. In a copy from 1892, an unnamed author described the drink as 'a curious liqueur composed from rum and lime juice.' Another reference to the liqueur crops up in an article entitled 'Falernum' that appeared in *The Philadelphia Inquirer* on 2 August 1896. This time we're treated to an actual recipe, which basically conforms to classic punch ratios (though it switches the ratio of sour and sweet, making for a kind of punch-liqueur):

*1 Part Lime Juice, 2 Parts Sugar Syrup, 3 Parts Rum, 4 Parts Water. Add almonds (almond extract) and allow the mixture to rest for a week. After resting bottle and serve over cracked ice with a teaspoon of wormwood bitters or substitute good quality bitters.*

During my research of the history of the Corn 'n' Oil cocktail, the more I read, the more it struck me that this drink is in fact a recipe for falernum – a recipe for falernum that, paradoxically, *contains* falernum.

Which rather begs the question – where the hell did the name Corn 'n' Oil come from? Well, most bartenders agree that the oil part of the name comes from the practice of floating black rum or bitters on top of the drink to simulate an oil spill. But nobody has a clue where the 'corn' part came from, so it doesn't tend to get mentioned. Nobody *had* a clue, I should say…

Barbados, like most of the Caribbean colonies, had become devoutly religious by the 19th century. This was partly thanks to frequent visits from European missionaries, and partly because the brutality of colonial life unequivocally proved the existence of the Devil, so surely there had to be a God too, right? Falernum liqueur may have gotten its name via one of these missionaries or some other, equally learned individual, as it sounds suspiciously close to the legendary Falernian wine that was produced on the slopes of Mount Falernus during the time of Jesus.

I tell you this because an ecclesiastical naming policy may have crept into the christening of the Corn 'n' Oil cocktail too. An extensive snoop around The Bible uncovers this passage from Deuteronomy: 'That I will give you the rain of your land in His due season, the first rain and the latter rain, that thou mayest gather in thy corn, and thy wine, and thine oil.'

Whether you take the 'wine' part to mean the rum or the falernum, all that is required to complete God's trio of flavours is the corn and the oil. So there you have it: Corn 'n' Oil – the alcoholic equivalent of manna from heaven.

# FALERNIAN WINE

250 ml/8½ fl. oz. Water
250 ml/8½ fl. oz. Doorly's XO Rum
125 ml/4¼ fl. oz. Wormwood & Almond Syrup (see opposite)
125 ml/4¼ fl. oz. Clarified Lime Juice (see pages 46–8)

Mix the ingredients together and store in the fridge for up to a month.
To serve, put a lump of ice in a rocks glass or wine glass and spritz the inside of
the glass with lime zest oils, discarding the zest. Pour 100 ml/3⅓ fl. oz. of chilled
Falernian Wine into the glass and serve.

Falernian wine was a cult wine during Roman times, mostly on account of its legendary strength, but it hasn't been produced for centuries. Historical texts suggest that it was a late harvest style, meaning it had more concentrated sugars and the potential for super-boozy ferments. Pliny the Elder (23–79 AD), the eminent Roman author and philosopher, alluded to this when he noted, 'It is the only wine that takes light when a flame is applied to it.' Now I don't know about you, but I can't recall the last time I saw a glass of wine on fire.

My recipe for Falernian Wine is in fact more of a recipe for falernum, as it was known in the 19th century, but it aims to balance sweetness, acidity and alcoholic kick in such a way that it might (with a little creative licence) be similar to the Falernian wines of Roman times.

The first commercial brand of falernum was manufactured in 1890 by John D. Taylor of Bridgetown, Barbados and sold under the brand name Velvet Falernum (it's still made today by the Foursquare Distillery in Barbados). Taylor was effectively bottling a punch, which, aside from being an astute commercial endeavour, would naturally result in some dumbing

down of the ingredients for the sake of shelf life and product stability. What once was a muddy infusion of lime juice, rum, sugar and almonds soon became a clove, pimento and lime-peel-flavoured syrup. While it lacked the freshness of the traditional falernum punch, it more than made up for it in terms of consistency.

I suspect that the people of Barbados still pined for old-style falernum punch, however, so they mixed themselves one using classic ratios, but instead of using sugar and almond extract, they used the newly available, pre-bottled falernum liqueur. This new drink could hardly be called falernum, since it contained Velvet Falernum, so the Corn 'n' Oil was born.

To make my Falernian Wine, I'm using a homemade wormwood and almond syrup made from a base of high-ester Jamaican rum. When assembling the cocktail, this syrup is mixed with an aged Barbados rum, clarified lime juice and water. The cocktail is served chilled from the fridge and simply poured over a large chunk of ice.

The ABV of the cocktail is approximately 18.5 per cent when the drink is first poured, which puts it in line with some of the strongest fortified wines available today.

# WORMWOOD & ALMOND SYRUP

15 G/½ OZ. RAW ALMONDS
100 ML/3½ FL. OZ. WRAY & NEPHEW OVERPROOF RUM (*or other* OVERPROOF WHITE RUM)
2 G/¹⁄₁₆ OZ. DRIED WORMWOOD

*Makes 200 ml/6¾ fl. oz.*

Blanch the almonds in boiling water for 1 minute, then mix them with the rum
and wormwood and store in a sealed mason jar for a week. Strain the infusion through
a muslin/cheesecloth filter, then mix with the sugar and reserve.

# GUNFIRE

150 ML/5 FL. OZ. HOT BLACK TEA
15 G/½ OZ. DEMERARA SUGAR
40 ML/1⅓ FL. OZ. PUSSER'S GUNPOWDER-STRENGTH RUM

Add the tea and sugar to a large-handled glass and stir to dissolve the sugar.
Add the rum in last, give another stir, then serve.

There is a long and rich history of drinking in the military and it's not too difficult to understand why: extended periods spent away from family and home, poor-quality food, constant fear of death, and the underlying sense that you may be required to kill someone in the not too distant future. A good drink can serve as a welcome panacea to all of the above and more.

For over 300 years the British Royal Navy served a rum ration, a practice that only ended in 1970. And while alcohol may not be as widely administered as it once was, there still exists a small catalogue of mixed drinks born out of mankind's proclivity to wage war.

Pretty much all of these drinks have two things in common: they are made from whatever ingredients are close at hand (and in the military that doesn't leave you with many options) and they all have the letter 'g' in their title: Gin & Tonic (yes, it is technically a cocktail), the Gimlet (stronger than you think it is), Pink Gin (stronger still), Grog (prone to dramatic variance) and Gunfire.

Gunfire is perhaps the best example of a cocktail made from ingredients foraged out of a mess tent or purser's (or pusser's) storeroom: rum, sugar and tea.

This drink was traditionally warmed up and served on Christmas Day. If you were a sailor who was unfortunate enough to be on tour or stationed at a military base during the festive period,

whether you found yourself in a hot climate or a cold one, Gunfire, traditionally at least (and I do not speak for the modern drinking habits of the armed forces), is what you would be sipping on.

And it really is this simple: a good slug of navy rum, topped up with warm sweetened tea.

Hardly mixology's finest moment, but that's not really the point. What's interesting here is the kind of forced innovation that occurs when one is faced with the conflicting desire to drink some alcohol but wishing to avoid the burn of neat spirits. Mixing drinks is the solution, and cocktails are the facilitator of strong alcohol consumption in a more civilised and measured way. The circumstances of a drink's creation also encourages us to think about the context in which a cocktail should be consumed. Clearly this is not a drink for a warm summer afternoon, but if I – for some bizarre reason – found myself at sea on a cold winter's evening, I'm not sure I could think of a more appropriate mixture to be sipping on.

From a cocktail genetics point of view, you only need to throw a squeeze of lemon into a Gunfire and you have yourself all the ingredients of a basic rum and tea-based punch. Without the lemon, the tannins of the tea are more pronounced, and I've found that the best way around them is just to load more sugar in until it becomes palatable.

# FERMEN-TEA PUNCH

35 ML/1¼ FL. OZ. CHAIRMAN'S RESERVE RUM
60 ML/2 FL. OZ. ASSAM KOMBUCHA (*see opposite*)
10 ML/⅓ FL. OZ. SUGAR SYRUP (*1:1 ratio – see page 32*)
50 ML/1⅔ FL. OZ. SODA WATER

Add all the ingredients to a chilled highball glass and stir over ice.

**Note:** Due to the unpredictable nature of kombucha brewing, you may need to adjust the quantity of sugar syrup to balance the acidity of your drink.

Rum and tea are unlikely to catch on as a pairing any time soon, unless they are in a punch bowl and accompanied by citrus, spices and sugar. That grassy, tannic flavour of tea is one of the great flavours of the world – it works brilliantly with gin, and green tea is a great match for vodka and malt whisky. But it really doesn't pair well with rum. Well, at least not in its conventional format. But what if there was a different way to brew tea, which introduced citric elements, sweetness, and some additional body? Could an ingredient like that be a match for rum?

Kombucha is fermented product that is made through the actions of a symbiotic colony of bacteria and yeast (SCOBY) on sweetened tea. Sometimes kombucha has additional fruit or herbs added to it; other times it's just tea, sugar and the SCOBY. The SCOBY is actually the reason why a lot of people mistakenly think kombucha is made from mushrooms, because the mass of SCOBY that floats on top of the ferment looks a bit like a mushroom cap. Well, it kind of is a mushroom cap in the sense that yeast is a fungus. But no, it's tea that is the main base of kombucha, and it'll be tea that we use to create a delicious new version of the Gunfire cocktail.

Kombucha can be made from any tea and the Gunfire cocktail can be made from any type of rum. That means there are lots of potential combinations of rum and tea, some of which will naturally work better than others. To get to the bottom of this, I made three batches of kombucha from a base of Assam, oolong and sencha tea, and tasted them alongside aged and unaged rums that varied in their production method, from heavy pot-still through to light column-still, as well as agricole variants.

Of course, certain teas paired better with certain types of rum: the grassiness of the green tea (sencha) kombucha combined nicely with the vegetal and soft tropical notes of an unnamed rhum agricole. On the other end of the scale, the nuttiness of the oolong kombucha paired nicely with light, Cuban-style rums such as Havana Club and Bacardi. But after much experimentation, I opted for an Assam kombucha mixed with an aged, blended rum. When using black tea, the kombucha offers fruity esters that are reminiscent of a good pot-still rum while the tannin from the tea simulates the effect of barrel ageing. The two combine seamlessly, resulting in one of the best rum highballs I can possibly imagine.

## ASSAM KOMBUCHA

18 G/⅔ OZ. ASSAM TEA
200 ML/6¾ FL. OZ. COLD WATER
1.7 LITRES/QUARTS BOILING WATER
150 G/5¼ OZ. SUGAR
1 X 80-G/2¾-OZ. KOMBUCHA SCOBY (*see page 44*)

*Makes 2 litres/2.1 quarts*

In a large jug/pitcher mix the tea, cold water, boiling water and sugar (in that order). Allow the liquid to cool for a couple of hours until it reaches 25°C/77°F. Strain the liquid into a 2-litre/2.1-quart sterilised kombucha or mason jar. Add the SCOBY to the mixture and cover but don't seal the jar. Leave it to ferment for 10–14 days. Strain the liquid into clean bottles and refrigerate for at least a week. Kombucha has an almost limitless lifespan when kept cold.

# RUM SWIZZLE

40 ML/1⅓ FL. OZ. SMITH & CROSS RUM
50 ML/1⅔ FL. OZ. PINEAPPLE JUICE
15 ML/½ FL. OZ. LIME JUICE
10 ML/⅓ FL. OZ. SUGAR SYRUP (*see page 32*)
2 DASHES ANGOSTURA BITTERS

Add all of the ingredients to a rocks glass or highball and fill with plenty of crushed ice. Swizzle for 10 seconds, then garnish with fresh mint and a slice of lime.

Swizzles are a family of sour-style drinks that are related to punches but are prepared with crushed ice and customarily 'swizzled' using a swizzle stick. A true swizzle stick is cut from an evergreen tree that goes by the Latin name *Quararibea turbinata*, but is known colloquially as the 'swizzlestick tree'. The lateral branches of the tree fork in clusters of five or six and at 90 degrees to the secondary branches, and once trimmed to size they form a perfectly proportioned, natural stirring tool – thanks, nature!

Swizzling has its origins in Caribbean and Central American food preparation, probably originating from the practice of stirring flasks of batter and dough with paddles, or from the traditional Mexican *molinillo* whisks that are used in the preparation of hot chocolate. It's unclear where the word 'swizzle' comes from, or whether the tree or the drink was the first to be named. One journalist from *The Southern Magazine* had this to say of the drink in 1894: 'Its name is probably derived from the "swizzle stick" or the name of the "swizzle stick" is derived from the "swizzle", upon which point the authorities are not clear.'

The first literary references suggest that 'swizzles' were common in the West Indies by the 1840s, which actually makes the swizzle one of the oldest families of mixed drinks there is after punches and juleps. I've heard it said (but I don't agree) that the forerunner to the swizzle was the switchel, a non-alcoholic drink comprising vinegar, water and spices, which was popular during the North American colonial period.

The 1909 book *Beverages, Past and Present: An Historical Sketch of Their Production* by Edward Randolph Emerson, informs us that a 'swizzle is composed of six parts of water to one part of rum and an aromatic flavouring'. The last part leaves the recipe rather open-ended, since an aromatic flavouring could constitute any ingredient that has an aroma. This gives swizzlers plenty of creative licence to experiment with whatever fruit or herbs they see fit, but a combination of pineapple juice and citrus seems to be the most commonly agreed upon contemporary modifier.

This is especially true if you are mixing a Bermudan Rum Swizzle. More than anywhere, the swizzle seems to have found its home in Bermuda. And yet, in spite of the tropical connotations of Bermuda, what with its shorts and its triangles, this temperate Atlantic island has neither swizzlestick trees nor a pineapple pit. Indeed, Bermuda is more like a slice of rural England (that just so happens to have been dropped 1000 km/620 miles from the nearest sensible-sized chunk of land) than a sultry paradise.

Swizzles can easily be made with a bar spoon, but if you can get hold of a real swizzlestick, you'll not regret it, as their natural shape generates unparalleled turmoil between liquid and ice. The trick is to submerge the spiky end of the stick in the iced cocktail, then hold the stick between the palms of your hands. In this way, the stick rotates back and forth quickly when you rub your hands together, generating lots of froth (thanks mostly to the pineapple juice) and rapid chilling.

# SWIZZLE TWIST

50 ML/1⅔ FL. OZ. Pineapple Rum (*see below*) • 20 ML/⅔ FL. OZ. Grapefruit Juice
10 ML/⅓ FL. OZ. Lime Juice • 10 ML/⅓ FL. OZ. Sugar Syrup (*see page 32*)

Combine all of the ingredients into a rocks glass and swizzle with crushed ice. Garnish
liberally with cubes of caramelised, rum-infused pineapple and pineapple leaves.

## PINEAPPLE RUM

500 G/18 OZ. Pineapple Diced into 1-CM/⅓-inch Chunks (*approx. 3 pineapples*)
700 ML/24 FL. OZ. Extra-Aged Jamaican Pot-Still Rum (Hampden *or* Worthy Park)
100 G/3½ OZ. Sugar • 250 G/9 OZ. Pineapple Husk Spirit (*see below*)

Macerate the pineapple flesh in the rum for a minimum of 2 weeks. This process can be sped up by heating the macerate (use a ziplock bag and water bath set to 50°C/122°F), but I personally don't like the slightly 'cooked' note that it imparts on the spirit.

Once infused, strain the liquid and reserve the chunks of pineapple. Sweeten the spirit with the sugar and mix with the Pineapple Husk Spirit at a ratio of roughly 3:1 (adjust according to your tastes).

Caramelise your rum-infused pineapple chunks for 5 minutes in a frying pan/skillet with a few teaspoons of sugar.

## PINEAPPLE HUSK SPIRIT

3 Large Pineapples • 700 ML/24 FL. OZ. Unaged Rum

Trim the leaves of the pineapples and reserve them for garnishing. Carefully slice the husk/bark off the pineapple, leaving as much of the fruit behind as possible.

Slice the bark into small pieces and mix with the rum. Distill the mixture in your chosen distillation apparatus (see pages 48–9). For this process, I used a rotary evaporator, which, due to its low operating temperature, produces a fragrant, grassy spirit. It should yield around 500 ml/ 17 fl. oz. of high-strength pineapple husk spirit.

When you're mixing up a Rum Swizzle, more than any of the other ingredients it'll be the pineapple juice that defines the quality of the finished serve. If you're using cartoned juice from concentrate, the drink will probably taste pretty bad regardless of which rum you use or how balanced it is. Good-quality pressed pineapple juice is preferable, but not always easy to get hold of. Juicing your own is the only guaranteed pathway to success, but it's a messy process and requires you to have a juicer at home. The only other option available to you is to redistill unaged rum alongside shredded pineapple bark, then macerate pineapple flesh into the resulting spirit, thus creating your very own pineapple-flavoured rum with which to mix the ultimate swizzle cocktail – easy, eh?

Sustainability is a hot topic in the bar world these days. It's not enough to make great-tasting drinks any more; the modern bar must keep a close watch on their

methods and processes to ensure that they are providing a sustainable offering that continually challenges itself to limit its environmental impact. Some simple practices that everyone can adopt is to refuse plastic straws and demand paper-, pasta- or vegetable-based straws instead. Another strategy (pioneered by my good friends at Trash Tiki) aims to minimise landfill waste by using the bits of ingredients we normally chuck away. Everything from spent lemon husks to avocado stones are up for grabs, the trick being to not just utilise them but to make drinks that taste good out of them, too.

Tiki is perhaps the best category of cocktails in which to champion sustainability. These drinks often contain potent flavours and call for lots of ingredients. A few drops of banana-skin bitters in a Mai Tai is unlikely to turn heads like it would in a Martini.

My pineapple rum is based loosely on Plantation Pineapple Rum (AKA Stiggin's Fancy), the drink of choice for Mr Stiggins in Charles Dickens's *The Pickwick Papers*. According to booze historian David Wondrich, Dickens's cellar was known to contain a stock of 'fine old pine-apple rum'. I always assumed the 'pine-apple' part referred to a high-ester style Jamaican rum (which has a tendency to smell of pineapple), but since the flavour pairs so well with rum, who am I to argue?

My finished Swizzle Twist calls for both lime juice and grapefruit juice as souring components. I find that the grapefruit juice actually amplifies some of the tropical notes in the rum, whereas lime has a tendency to just make things taste of lime! The two in concert give the drink the right level of acidity along with a 'totally tropical taste'.

# WHISKY

# BLUE BLAZER

. . . . . . . . . . . . . . . . . . . . . . . . . . . . . . . . . . . . . . . . . . . . . . . . . . . . . . . . . . . . . . . . . . . . . .

120 ML/4 FL. OZ. DEWAR'S 12-YEAR-OLD BLENDED SCOTCH WHISKY
120 ML/4 FL. OZ. BOILING WATER
10 G/⅓ OZ. SUGAR

*Makes 2*

Although this drink can be made using steel jugs/pitchers (the kind that might be used for steaming milk in a café) you will find it easier and safer to use large tankards with nice, long handles.

Preheat both tankards with hot water, then put the whisky in one tankard and the boiling water and sugar in the other. Light the whisky (this may take a couple of attempts if the whisky is cold) and swirl it around in the tankard to encourage a good flame. Pour the burning whisky into the tankard with the water. Then pour back, repeating the process. As the liquids warm, the flames will become more ferocious.

Practice will allow you to increase the distance between vessels when pouring, giving the effect of a long, blue-flamed waterfall. You can snuff out the flame at any time by covering the flaming vessel with the base of the other vessel. Pour into a handled glass and serve with a twist of lemon peel.

The 19th-century mixologist was considered a master of all things delicious and fancy. But 'fancy' in the 1800s didn't mean dry ice and strips of orange zest cut with pinking shears. The original mixologists – or should I say mixologist (singular)? – had considerably more theatrical tricks up their sleeves and it's in part thanks to these feats of alcohol entertainment that the art of bartending achieved celebrity status.

Jeremiah 'Jerry' P. Thomas is the undisputed father of American mixology. As a travelling bartender he worked/performed across dozens of bars through the 1850s in St Louis, Chicago, Charleston, New Orleans and New York. His *Bar-Tender's Guide* (alternately titled *How to Mix Drinks* or *The Bon-Vivant's Companion*), published in 1862, was the first cocktail book written by a US author, and the first book to successfully categorise the vast array of mixed drinks that had been born out of the early 19th century. Most of Thomas's category systems are still in use today, and the creation of numerous classic cocktails are credited to him as well.

Perhaps his most famous creation is the Blue Blazer, which he developed while working at the El Dorado gambling saloon in San Francisco. Using a set of large, solid-silver mugs, Thomas would 'throw' flaming slugs of burning Scotch between the vessels to an audience of mesmerised patrons. In the *Bar-Tender's Guide*, Thomas noted that any patrons witnessing the display, 'would naturally come to the conclusion that it was a nectar for Pluto [god of the underworld] rather than Bacchus'.

When I opened my first London bar back in 2009, we included a Blazer on the menu. Being a speakeasy kind of place, where bartenders wore bow ties and guests read menus by candlelight, the Blue Blazer fitted in rather well. But the bar was like a rabbit warren, meaning that only around 20 guests at any one time had a clear view of the drink's preparation. This was problematic in so far as the Blue Blazer was concerned, since much of the enjoyment of the drink can be taken in admiring the knife-edge spectacle of its preparation. So we took to pouring Blazers at the table. That combination of danger and the promise of alcohol was enough to excite even the most sceptical of guests, but for me it offered a taste of just how mind-blowing such a performance must have seemed 150 years ago.

. . . . . . . . . . . . . . . . . . . . . . . . . . . . . . . . . . . . . . . . . . . . . . . . . . . . . . . . . . . . . . . . . . . . . .

# NAVAL BLAZER

110 ML/3¾ FL. OZ. SMITH & CROSS RUM (*or another aged pot-still rum*)

10 ML/⅓ FL. OZ. ARDBEG 10 SCOTCH WHISKY

50 ML/1⅔ FL. OZ. MANZANILLA SHERRY

50 ML/1⅔ FL. OZ. BOILING WATER

10 ML/⅓ FL. OZ. BALSAMIC VINEGAR

20 G/⅔ OZ. DEMERARA SUGAR

*Makes 2*

Follow the same instructions as for the Blue Blazer (see page 146) ensuring that you preheat your vessels. Mix the sherry, water, vinegar and sugar in one vessel and the rum and whisky in the other.

Ignite the rum vessel and then carefully pour the liquids between each vessel, lengthening pours as you go.

Pour the flaming liquid into a heatproof mug or glass and briefly toast some liquorice/licorice on a skewer. Douse the liquorice/licorice in the drink and snuff the flame out. Swirl the contents of the glass and allow it to cool for a few minutes before drinking.

There's more to Blazers than just theatre. The 'throwing' action aerates the drink, while combustion triggers thousands of tiny flavour-contributing explosions amongst the vaporised alcohol. The drink is irreversibly altered. It's difficult to describe the effect of these changes on the palate, but certainly there's an inherent spiciness to a good Blazer and a balanced bitterness brought about by caramelisation of sugars. The effect on your state of well-being is easier to express, as this heady concoction, which sits somewhere between hot Champagne and whisky, energises and uplifts even the darkest of moods.

The simplicity of the ingredients belie the multi-sensory complexity of the serve. And the basic ratio of Scotch, sugar and water also leaves the Blazer open to a range of modification strategies. My Naval Blazer recipe aims to harness the spice and depth of the classic version and amplify them with a few choice ingredients that steer the drink in a more maritime direction (hence the name). And because of this, I'm also taking a bold move and switching the Scotch for rum.

Good-quality molasses-based rum would have been hard to come by during Jerry Thomas's time, but I figure that if it were available to him, he might have opted to use it in place of whisky. At the risk of falling into the trap of rum and pirate clichés, a flaming liquid being poured between metal tankards does seems to speak more of rum and sailors than it does whisky and bagpipers. I also think that the bittersweet effervescence of a well-constructed Blazer is more matched to the flavour profile of a rich, tropical-scented pot-still rum than it is to the subtle honey and soft fruit qualities of Scotch. That said, I am using a small 'seasoning' of peated single malt to impart a gentle 'sooty' quality to the drink.

Now that we're fully entangled in the pirate/nautical theme, I'm adding two further modifiers that continue with the same theme. The first is manzanilla sherry, which possesses that wonderful salinity reminiscent of the ocean. The second is balsamic vinegar, which will contribute gentle, fermented, 'funk' flavours along with dark, spiced fruit.

To garnish, I pour the drink into a heatproof mug and briefly toast liquorice/licorice over the flames before dousing them into the cocktail. The chief flavour of liquorice/licorice is fennel seed, but due to its rich treacle-like composition, it reminds me a lot of molasses – the base material of many rums.

# VIEUX CARRÉ

25 ML/¾ FL. OZ. VSOP COGNAC
25 ML/¾ FL. OZ. RITTENHOUSE RYE
25 ML/¾ FL. OZ. MARTINI ROSSO
5 ML/1 TEASPOON BENEDICTINE
1 DASH PEYCHAUD'S BITTERS
1 DASH ANGOSTURA BITTERS

Add the ingredients to a mixing beaker and stir over cubed ice for a minute.
Strain into a rocks glass filled with ice. Garnish with a twist of lemon peel.
**Note**: The original recipe suggests optionally garnishing with a slice of pineapple
and a cherry. The Carousel Bar is loyal to this… I'm not a fan.

Take a stroll along New Orleans' famed Bourbon Street and it's mostly karaoke bars, strip clubs and signs declaring 'Huge-ass beers' that light up the sidewalk. Then there's the smell of damp, fermenting street grime and discarded plastic alco-slushy cups that crunch under your feet. These days it can be difficult to imagine how the French Quarter once housed some of the best bars and most innovative bartenders in the world, and was responsible for the creation of more classic cocktails than any other neighbourhood on the planet.

Also known to locals as the Vieux Carré (Old Square), the French Quarter is still home to some fantastic old bars (including the oldest bar in America, which, by the way, is *not* fantastic). Contrary to the name, the oldest buildings in the French Quarter were in fact built during the Spanish occupation (1762–1802), which saw fires in 1788 and 1794 destroy the 'first generation' French Creole properties.

The majority of the buildings we see today were raised during the early part of the 19th century after the US had taken possession of this territory. At that time, Mississippi steamboats facilitated excellent trade routes with the northerly states, and the Gulf of Mexico offered a gateway to transatlantic trading, making New Orleans the largest port in the south. The city's population grew at a staggering rate through the 19th century, from 17,000 to 170,000 in the space of 50 years. With it came extraordinary wealth, which created a need for fancy hotels and decadent bars.

One such hotel was the Commercial, which was founded by Antonio Monteleone on the corner of Royal and Chartres Streets in 1886. This French Quarter hotel has remained in the Monteleone family ever since, undergoing various and numerous expansions, before being mostly demolished and rebuilt into its current state in 1954. Perhaps the most notable feature of the hotel is the Carousel Bar, which was originally built in 1949. The bar is a circular 'island' style, seating 25 guests, and it rotates at a rate of one revolution every 15 minutes – slow enough so you don't get dizzy but fast enough to disorientate you (especially after a few cocktails).

Speaking of cocktails, it was an earlier, non-rotating, iteration of the Carousel Bar, where the Vieux Carré was first mixed. Walter Bergeron was the head bartender there during the 1930s, and following the drink's creation, the cocktail featured in the 1937 publication *Famous New Orleans Drinks and how to mix 'em*.

In structure, the drink sits somewhere between a Manhattan and a Sazerac. There are some provocative pairings of ingredients here, though: rye does battle with Cognac and two varieties of bitters have a face-off. In many ways it is both a Manhattan and a Sazerac in the same glass, where the absinthe has been replaced with Benedictine. That last part is a critical element to the success of the drink, however, because it brings sweetness and harmonises the floral, fruity Cognac with the spice of the rye.

# APERITIF LOUISIANE

500 ML/17 FL. OZ. VSOP COGNAC • 200 ML/6¾ FL. OZ. SEMI-SWEET RIESLING WINE

### BITTER
2 G/⅛ OZ. GENTIAN ROOT • 1 G/1/16 OZ. WORMWOOD

### FRUITY
25 G/1 OZ. DEHYDRATED STRAWBERRY • 50 G/1¾ OZ. DRIED CHERRY

### AROMATIC
5 G/⅙ OZ. PIMENTO BERRIES • 1 WHOLE STAR ANISE • 5 WHOLE CLOVES
1 SPLIT VANILLA POD/BEAN

### EARTHY
15 G/½ OZ. FENNEL SEEDS • 10 G/⅓ OZ. THYME LEAVES • 10 G/⅓ OZ. DANDELION ROOT
3 G/⅛ OZ. GRATED NUTMEG • 5 G/⅙ OZ. CACAO NIBS
5 G/⅙ OZ. GRATED TAMARIND • 5 G/⅙ OZ. WHOLE BLACK PEPPERCORNS

### SWEET
75 ML/2½ FL. OZ. MAPLE SYRUP

*Makes 1 × 700-ml/24-fl. oz. bottle*

Take a mason jar and add to it all of the ingredients except the wine and maple syrup. Close the lid tightly and allow the ingredients to macerate for approximately 6 weeks, shaking occasionally. Once fully infused, strain the liquid through a muslin/cheesecloth filter then add the wine, sweeten with maple syrup and re-bottle. Store in the fridge and pour directly over ice to serve. If you wish, you can lengthen the cocktail with soda water, tonic water, ginger beer or lemonade.

Selecting ingredients and balancing flavour is large part of the joy of mixing drinks. But when making a cocktail like a Vieux Carré, with its numerous red and brown-coloured ingredients, my thoughts often turn to simpler cocktails that can be poured straight from just one bottle! I'm talking about pre-mixed products like Campari, Aperol and Pimm's, where the hard work of balancing sugar, bitter and aromatic flavourings is all done for you.

Although, on paper, a Vieux Carré seems like a strong cocktail, and calls for a lot of boozy ingredients, by the time it's diluted with ice it actually sits more in the realms of a mid-strength bittersweet aperitif. And like the brands that I have already mentioned, it should stimulate on that same level, as a pre-dinner herbal palate awakener. The fruit and oak characteristics of Cognac; the spice of rye; the herbal and sweet qualities of Italian vermouth and Benedictine; and the dark and fragrant properties of not one, but two types of bitters. The Vieux Carré is a marvel of mixology that flies in the face of the adage that simple is always better. But when you consider that five out of the six ingredients are made from a spirit base, and all that really distinguishes them is what they have been flavoured with, a nifty shortcut to the end point wouldn't be unwelcome.

So this bodes the question: could you infuse a spirit and wine mixture with all of the flavours that are present in a Vieux Carré and create an aperitif cocktail that embodies all the classic cocktail flavours of New Orleans?

I think you can. And I think, with some careful measuring, it can be done in two steps, starting with a simple maceration of herbs, fruits and spices into wine and brandy, and finishing with a touch of sweetening.

My ingredients can be split broadly between five camps of flavour: bitter, fruity, aromatic, earthy and sweet. I have listed them in these groups so as to help you identify how the marriage of these ingredients have been established. Listing them this way will also help you to adjust or swap out ingredients if you are inclined to do so.

With Cognac as a base (providing fruit, perfume and oak notes) and wine lengthening the aperitif out (while giving citric, fruit and floral aromas) the drink is beefed up by the addition of bitter herbs and roots alongside deep, earthy spice. This goes some way to simulating the effect of the (missing) rye whisky and, of course, the bitters. The aromatic ingredients provide some of the same aromas you might expect to find in bitters but also in vermouth, while the fruit components bind together those rich spices with the light, fruity

flavours of the wine. I choose to sweeten with maple syrup, which is suggestive of American whiskey and all the caramel and toffee flavours that it would normally bring to a drink. For the wine component I'm using a semi-sweet German Riesling wine. Remember that even sweet vermouths are made from a base of white wine, and this low-acidity style plays nicely with the Cognac.

The development of this drink was no different from the development of a marketable bottled cocktail product. It involved creating separate infusions of every ingredient, then blending them together in varying proportions until balance was achieved, then adjusting weights and ratios to accommodate. This is my recipe for Aperitif Louisiane, but it also serves as a basic set of instructions on how to manufacture any bottled aperitif-style cocktail.

# RUSTY NAIL

40 ML / 1⅓ FL. OZ DEWAR'S 12-YEAR-OLD SCOTCH WHISKY
20 ML / ⅔ FL. OZ. DRAMBUIE

Take a big lump of ice, pop it in a rocks glass, then pour the whisky and Drambuie over the top and stir well for a minute. That's it.

If you can't make a Rusty Nail taste good it's probably time to give up on this mixology thing. After all, a drink that comprises only two ingredients, where one of them is Scotch whisky and the other is Scotch whisky that's been sweetened and had herbal flavours added to it ought to be simple enough to balance to anyone's palate. Like it sweeter? Add more Drambuie. Like it dryer? Use less Drambuie. Only those people born with a complete inability to understand why they do or do not like a flavour or with an inability to change things appropriately will stand a chance at messing this one up.

So what is this Drambuie stuff? In the most basic sense it's a whisky liqueur, flavoured with heather honey, a bunch of other herbs and exotic spices. The name Drambuie is derived from Scots Gaelic *an dram buidheach* and means 'the drink that satisfies'. By the light of an open fire on a cold Scottish evening, it'll do just that.

The accepted history of this product is a tale of Scottish spirit seasoned liberally with various fantastical components. It begins with Bonnie Prince Charlie (Charles Edward Stuart) aka the Young Pretender, whose failed Jacobite uprising of 1745 left him in exile on the Isle of Skye rather than sitting on the thrones of England, Scotland, Ireland and France. With little left to occupy his time, Charlie became acquainted with the noble arts of wenching and drinking – French brandy being his preferred tipple. As was common amongst the nobility of that time, Bonnie Prince Charlie had his own recipe for a curative liqueur, which would have been formulated for him by a personal physician or apothecary. The story goes that Charles shared the recipe for his tonic with his friend Captain John MacKinnon in 1746, though Drambuie's testimony on this matter has changed at least twice over the years. Early-19th-century advertising states it was 'a follower of Prince Charlie' that brought the spirit to Scotland, then later a 'gentleman of the bodyguard of Prince Charlie'.

The truth is that nobody really knows how John MacKinnon came to acquire the recipe, but most people agree that it was probably brandy-based in the first instance. The recipe remained a MacKinnon family secret for some 150 years, then was passed on to the Ross family who ran the Broadford Hotel on the Isle of Skye. The Rosses registered the trademark for Drambuie in 1893. Production later moved to Edinburgh and the company was bought by Malcolm MacKinnon (no relation to the other MacKinnons in this tale), in whose family it has remained ever since.

These days, Drambuie has a reputation for being a divisive liqueur. I have friends and colleagues who love it and others who hate it, but very few who sit on the fence. The general rule of thumb, so much as I can tell, is if you're not averse to very sweet things, you will get along with it just fine. This, then, is where the Rusty Nail comes into its own. A simple tweak of the ratios will get you where you want to be in terms of sweetness and herbal lift.

# RUSTEN SPIKER

700 ML/24 FL. OZ. SINGLE MALT WHISKY AT 50 PER CENT ABV
(*adjust strength accordingly*)
20 G/¾ OZ. SILVER BIRCH BARK TEA • 15 G/½ OZ. FENNEL SEEDS
10 G/⅓ OZ. DRIED DOUGLAS FIR NEEDLES • 5 G/⅙ OZ. MACE BLADES
0.5 G/2 PINCHES SAFFRON • 175 G/6¼ OZ. HEATHER HONEY

Add all of the whisky and spices to a mason jar and seal. Leave to infuse for at least 1 week.
Strain the liquid through a fine tea strainer and warm the honey in a pot of hot water. Mix
the honey and whisky until fully incorporated. No need to mix with more whisky (unless
you wish) – simply pour over ice and garnish with birch bark and a sprig of rosemary

You may note that the whisky section of this volume is quite hands-on when it comes to DIY ingredients. Although I didn't set out to make it that way, it isn't unwarranted, due to the distinctiveness of flavour pairings we find in classic whisky cocktails. Many of these drinks call for whisky to be mixed with herbal liqueurs from well-established brands that are medicinal in their origin. You may also note that through broad commercialisation, some of these liqueurs have become a little sterile. But being of medicinal origin, there are countless texts that detail the manufacture of similar products that use natural ingredients and traditional preparation methods. With that in mind, and given the quality of ingredients available to the modern mixologist, it isn't difficult to develop vastly superior versions of *some* liqueurs.

Drambuie is a liqueur that is ready for renovation. And you needn't only think of this as a labour-intensive route to an improved cocktail. This recipe produces a spirit that can be enjoyed throughout the winter, after dinner, or at any other time that suits. I have fully 'winterised' this recipe by shaping it with flavours and flora that are common to the Nordic countries… I suspect that in winter they could do with a livener like this.

When you're developing a recipe for a whisky-based honey liqueur, the whisky and honey are all-important. Yes, this liqueur will be flavoured with Nordic herbs and other botanical ingredients too – and their selection and quantities are also important – but using cheap whisky or poor-quality honey will negatively impact flavour in a way that will be difficult to recover from. Atypically for a liqueur, Drambuie is bottled at 40 per cent ABV, so the same kind of potency as a blended whisky and many single malts. But if you use a 40 per cent spirit to make your liqueur, you will be bottling a product of less than 40 per cent ABV once you have added sweetening. The solution is to use a stronger whisky, which takes us into single malt and 'cask-strength' territory.

For the honey component, I suggest you to try a range before settling on one. I found From Field to Flower in London's Borough Market to be very open to tasting a bunch of styles before I settled on the right one – a heather honey from Norway. This honey was relatively light in colour, but with plenty of cool, floral aromatics that paint a powerful representation of the place.

For the herbal infusion, I'm using a small selection of hardy autumn/winter herbs alongside silver birch bark and Douglas fir needles. I've purposely chosen ingredients that are Nordic in origin and that impart characteristics sitting at the more herbal, woodsy and savoury end of the flavour spectrum. Bitterness is desirable in this liqueur, and the use of non-sweet seasonings is a tactic designed to counteract some of the sweetness that the honey will contribute, drying out the flavour and avoiding sickliness.

With regards to the silver birch bark tea, which imparts a noticeable bitterness as well as that warming smell of a sauna, make sure the birch tea that you source is made from the reddish-coloured phloem.

Oh, and just in case you hadn't worked it out already, *Rusten Spiker* is Norwegian for 'rusty nail'.

# BOULEVARDIER

40 ML/1⅓ FL. OZ. MAKER'S MARK BOURBON • 20 ML/⅔ FL. OZ. CAMPARI
20 ML/⅔ FL. OZ. MARTINI ROSSO

Add all of the ingredients to a mixing beaker and stir over cubed ice for at least 90 seconds.
Strain into a chilled coupe glass and garnish with a small twist of orange. You may like to add a
splash of water to the mixing beaker too – this helps to cut through the syrupy Campari and
lighten the drink a little.

If the recipe for this drink seems familiar, that's because it is. The Boulevardier is the American cousin of the Negroni, made from a base of American whiskey and named for an American… in France.

This drink, like many others, was created by Harry MacElhone of Harry's New York Bar in Paris. It is mentioned only briefly in his book *Barflies and Cocktails* (1927), not among the cocktail recipes, but rather in the epilogue that follows, which recounts the antics of his regular patrons: 'Now is the time for all good barflies to come to the aid of the party, since Erskine Gwynne crashed in with his Boulevardier Cocktail: ⅓ Campari, ⅓ Italian vermouth, ⅓ bourbon whisky.' Erskine Gwynne was a wealthy young journalist who came to Paris from New York, and in 1927 launched a literary magazine for posh men about town called – you guessed it – *The Boulevardier*.

On appearances this seems like a straightforward origin story: a famous cocktail bartender with his own written account of the drink's creation and a catchy name attributed to a known journalist... but there are just a couple of outstanding matters.

The first question that needs addressing is how did Harry MacElhone come to have bourbon in his bar in 1927? Prohibition did not exist in France at that time, of course, (except for absinthe, which was banned), but spirits production in the US had been on hold for nearly a decade, and the only whiskey produced there was for medical purposes. The only answer is that MacElhone had gathered quite a stock of the stuff prior to the 1920s and must have charged a high premium for drinks that contained it.

The second curiosity here is the drink itself. It shares more than a passing similarity to the Negroni, leading many drinks experts to conclude that it was based on the Negroni, which was invented in Florence sometime around 1919 or 1920. Harry MacElhone published an earlier book called *Harry's ABC of Mixing Cocktails* in 1919, but as one might expect, there's no mention of the Boulevardier or the Negroni in there. There's also no mention of the Negroni in *Barflies and Cocktails* (1927), and indeed you have to wait until 1959 and *Wake Up In Europe: a Book of Travel for Australians & New Zealanders* by Colin Simpson before we see the first mention of the Negroni in print.

However, looking at the 1922 reprint of *Harry's ABC of Mixing Cocktails*, we do encounter a new cocktail that contains equal parts whiskey, Campari and vermouth. In this instance, the drink is made with Canadian whiskey and French vermouth. The name of the drink is Old Pal. Incredibly, Harry attributes the creation of Old Pal to another American journalist living in Paris, as we can see with the credit: 'Recipe by "Sparrow" Robertson, Sporting Editor of the *New York Herald*, Paris.'

In summary, the whole thing is a bit of a mess. But messes are not uncommon where the documentation of alcohol is concerned. It goes without saying that a lot of what gets written about drinks is done so while the author is under the influence – yours truly being no exception. But taking all that we know about Harry's meddling with Campari, vermouth and whiskey in the 1920s, I think it's fair to say that both the Old Pal and the Boulevardier were created completely independently of the Negroni.

That leaves one final (rather important) question: is the Boulevardier a good drink?

Well, the great thing about using bourbon in place of gin is that, unlike the delicate juniper characteristics of the latter, the aged spirit is actually discernible in the finished drink. I like a Negroni as much as the next bartender with a tattoo of a bitters bottle on their neck, but picking out the gin in an equal-parts Negroni is nigh on impossible. Not so with a Boulevardier. That said, I still think it pragmatic to up the amount of bourbon a little to really let it shine. This shifts the cocktail further in the direction of a Manhattan. Indeed, if you were to draw a Venn diagram with circles that represented a Negroni and a Manhattan, the Boulevardier would sit in the intersection.

With that kind of pedigree behind it, it's quite puzzling that the Boulevardier hasn't progressed beyond the realms of the late-night, post-shift bartender-to-bartender order and into the domain of regular guests. Try it!

# BOULEVARDIER À LA RUE DAUNOU

40 ML/1⅓ FL. OZ. CHERRY-SMOKED BOURBON (*see below*)
20 ML/⅔ FL. OZ. CAMPARI
20 ML/⅔ FL. OZ MARTINI ROSSO
5 ML/1 TEASPOON LAGAVULIN 16-YEAR-OLD SCOTCH WHISKY
5 ML/1 TEASPOON PEDRO XIMENEZ SHERRY

You can smoke your bourbon using any of the techniques listed on pages 50–55. The trick, as always with smoking, is to saturate the spirit with smoke to make a concentrate, then dilute with unsmoked bourbon until you reach an acceptable intensity. This drink should be smoky, but it's essential that the fruit flavours balance the smoke.

Add all of the ingredients to a mixing beaker and stir over cubed ice for at least one minute. Strain into a coupe glass and garnish with a tobacco leaf.

It could be argued that you cannot truly replicate the flavour of a classic cocktail unless you also replicate the environment in which the cocktail was originally consumed. For the Batanga that might mean sweltering heat and plastic picnic tables. For the White Lady it would be a marble-topped bar and jazz piano. And for a cocktail invented in 1920s Paris? Well, a room full of cigarette smoke, of course!

Make no bones about it, if you were drinking a Boulevardier at Harry's in 1920, you were also drinking in a few hundred litres of smoke-filled air alongside it. The pipe would no doubt have been prevalent here too, but cigarette is a French word and the cigarette is synonymous with France – enjoyed by the great names of French creativity from Colette to Cocteau and Camus to Coco Chanel (who was a famous patron of Harry's). Indeed, Paris even boasts a Museum of Smoking, and has named a street after Jean Nicot, the 16th-century French diplomat whom nicotine was named for after he took tobacco leaves imported from America to Catherine de Medici to treat her migraines. (In truth, France's obsession with smoking is overstated these days, and the nation's per capita consumption is actually far lower than that of Russia, China or the Balkans.)

So the cultural history of France gives us good enough justification for smoking a Boulevardier cocktail, but hold that thought and also consider that this drink is made from a base of American spirit that pairs well with barbecues and an Italian aperitif that is flavoured with orange (an ingredient that also shares an affinity with smoke). Now we have ourselves a premise of a mixed drink that sounds altogether rather delicious.

Of course it's not cigarette or cigar smoke that I'll be smoking this drink with, as those products impart a rather well-documented toxicity that would be quite undesirable. I won't be using a tobacco infusion either, as toxins are readily extracted from tobacco and can become highly concentrated during maceration. Instead, I'm smoking a combination of peated whisky and cherry-wood smoke. The peat smoke from the whisky will bring about a sooty, phenolic aroma to the drink, while the cherry-wood smoke contributes lighter, fruitier notes. I'm also including a dash of PX sherry in my drink, which will give the flavour of dried fruits like sultanas/golden raisins and apricot. The overall effect will be reminiscent of moist, fruity tobacco, wafting through the bittersweet currents of a classic Boulevardier. And perhaps it will taste something like the original, served at Harry's New York Bar, 5 Rue Daunou, Paris.

# BOBBY BURNS

50 ML/1⅔ FL. OZ. DEWARS 15-YEAR-OLD SCOTCH WHISKY
25 ML/¾ FL. OZ. MARTINI ROSSO • 7.5 ML/1½ TEASPOONS BENEDICTINE

Add all of the ingredients to a mixing beaker and stir over cubed ice for 90 seconds. Strain into
a chilled coupe glass and garnish with a very small strip of orange zest.

It's widely recognised that this drink was named after the 18th-century Scottish poet Robert 'Rabbie' Burns. And who could be better deserving of a cocktail eponym than Scotland's national poet?

Contrary to the habits of literally *all* of my Scottish friends, Burns wasn't a heavy drinker. Much of his poetry was well lubricated however, with tales of John Barleycorn (the personification of both barley and the beverages made from it) and *usquabae* (Gaelic for 'whisky'). Whisky was indeed a subject of great sentiment to Burns, and while it's well known that the Ploughman Poet was a farmer, he also worked as an excise officer (or gauger), which naturally took him to some of Scotland's oldest and most legendary distilleries. Over 220 years have passed since his death, but the enjoyment of whisky is still strongly associated with Burns, and practised by many a non-whisky drinker each 25 January – Burns's birthday.

As for the cocktail, on the face of things this appears to be a cut-and-dried case. Like so many other cocktails, the first written reference to the drink was in Harry Craddock's *The Savoy Cocktail Book* (1930). Listed as a Bobby Burns, the drink calls for a Scotch and Italian vermouth base plus a dash of Benedictine. 'One of the very best Whisky cocktails,' Craddock wrote, and added, 'a very fast mover on St. Andrew's Day.'

There's just one tiny problem. Nobody ever refers to Robert Burns as Bobby Burns. *Rabbie* perhaps, but never Bobby. This (apparent) lackadaisical naming of Craddock's has had me wondering for years why you would name a cocktail after someone, but using the incorrect form of their name?

To get to the bottom of this it might, for once, be necessary to look forward rather than back. A year after the release of *The Savoy Cocktail Book*, the *Old Waldorf Bar Days* book by Albert Stevens Crockett was published. This book, which contained 'Four Hundred and Ninety One Appealing Appetisers and Salutary Potations', was an epitaph to New York's original Waldorf-Astoria Hotel, which was razed in 1929 to make way for the construction of the Empire State Building. With that in mind, we can assume that all of the drinks in the book existed prior to the closure of the hotel, including a drink that calls for Scotch and Italian vermouth and is finished with a dash of absinthe and orange bitters. Crockett calls this drink a Robert Burns. We can then assume that Craddock adapted this drink and in doing so changed Robert to Bobby.

The plot thickens, as Crockett includes the following notation: 'It may have been named after the celebrated Scotsman. Chances are, however, that it was christened in honour of a cigar salesman, who "bought" in the Bar.'

It turns out that Robert Burns was once a popular brand of cigar that had been about since the mid-1800s and was marketed nationally in the US from 1917 onwards. Perhaps the aforementioned salesman was called Robert Burns too, but it seems more plausible to me that he simply smoked a lot of his own product and the drink took its name from a cigar brand.

For me, this seems a more likely genesis than Craddock's earlier published recipe. But it still doesn't explain why Craddock changed the name to Bobby. Perhaps for the alliteration on Benedictine? Or simply to distinguish the drink from the Waldorf version?

Or maybe the most obvious explanation is the correct one: he named the drink after Bobby Burns – the American actor who appeared in over 200 movies between 1908 and 1952.

# BUCKY BURNS

45 ml/1½ fl. oz. Craigellachie 17-year-old Scotch Whisky
20 ml/⅔ fl. oz. Buckfast Tonic Wine
10 ml/⅓ fl. oz. Bræmble Liqueur

Add cubed ice to a mixing beaker then pour in all of the ingredients.
Stir for a minute, then strain into a chilled drinking horn.
Garnish with grapes, blackberries and a sprig of barley.

For a drink with such a strong connection to Scotland, the Bobby Burns has some decidedly non-Scottish themes to its history and construction. Just the minor issues that it was invented in New York by an American, uses a French liqueur and vermouth and is named after an American cigar brand. The only Scottish thing about it is the whisky. Given the strong association between this drink and Scotland, these truths don't sit well with me, so I set about developing a modified version of this classic that relies heavily on the flavours of Scotland.

Unfortunately, Scotland is not one of the great vermouth-producing nations of this world. In fact, at the time of writing only one brand exists and it's a dry vermouth. The Scottish are partial to the taste of herbal, botanical wines however, chiefly a highly caffeinated riff on vermouth called Buckfast Tonic Wine.

Buckfast was originally concocted in the 1800s by monks at Buckfast Abbey in Devon. The Abbey lost their licence to sell alcohol in 1927 (I don't know why this happened but wouldn't be surprised if 'Bucky' consumption had something to do with it), and since then the product's distribution was licensed out to a third party. I've never seen anyone in Devon drink Buckfast. I've never seen anyone drink it in the rest of England, either. But by golly do they drink it in Scotland. In fact, Buckfast has gained quite a reputation, particularly in Glasgow, for its association with violent crime. The *Guardian* newspaper described it in 2015 as a 'drink with almost supernatural powers of destruction'.

In inner-city Glasgow, Buckfast is colloquially known as 'wreck the hoose [sic] juice' and 'commotion lotion'.

Meanwhile, in Devon, the monks insist that their product contains nothing that would incite violent behaviour. But with Buckfast reportedly a significant factor in 40 per cent of arrests in Scotland, there is the possibility that Buckfast might be a little bit evil.

The good news is that it actually tastes rather good – like sweet vermouth, only sweeter. But with three times the caffeine content of Coca-Cola you will want to be using it sparingly, which is why it makes such a great cocktail modifier.

In place of Benedictine I'm using a Scottish liqueur called Bræmble. This product was brought to market by some pals of mine in 2017, headed up by the owners of Bramble cocktail bar in Edinburgh. Unsurprisingly, this liqueur is based on the Bramble cocktail, which is usually made from gin, citrus and crème de mûre (blackberry liqueur). The liqueur is not as sweet as you might imagine, however, and instead delivers dark forest fruits and a delicious drying quality.

Lastly, there's the whisky. Ask any Glaswegian 'ned' and they'll tell you that when you're going up against Buckfast you'll want some serious backup. That's why I'm calling in the big guns and using for Craigellachie 17. This is not cheap, but it is delicious, and through a combination of tropical fruits, light smoke and a muscular mouthfeel, it throws a solid right-hook at the Buckfast while the Bræmble explodes with fruit and florals.

# WHISKY MAC

45 ML/1½ FL. OZ. ABERFELDY 12-YEAR-OLD SCOTCH WHISKY

30 ML/1 FL. OZ. STONE'S ORIGINAL GINGER WINE

Add the ingredients to a rocks glass filled with ice and stir for a minute.
That's it.

There exists a very small category of mixed drinks that rarely appear on cocktail menus yet they are well known to virtually anyone who has ever picked up a glass of booze. These drinks require no introduction and to make a fuss over them would be to miss the point entirely. They are the corduroy of the drinks world (never out of fashion, never in fashion): familiar and accessible, but not appreciated enough. And just like corduroy, on the rare occasions that we do choose to try them out, we find them to be an altogether agreeable fit.

The Whisky Mac is one of these drinks. When was the last time you ordered one in a bar? You probably never have. But you are aware of it and you know what it tastes like – whisky and ginger.

Most recipes for a Whisky Mac state that you *must* use Stone's Original Ginger Wine as the ginger component of the cocktail. I doubt a Whisky Mac has ever been made with anything other than Stone's. For those of you who haven't tried Stone's Original, I can tell you that it's not quite a wine and not quite a liqueur.

It's made by fermenting a combination of overripe grapes and ginger, then fortifying it with spirit, sweetener and flavourings. Emphasis on the sweetener. At 13.9 per cent ABV it'll more likely be the sugar that gets you before the alcohol does. The flavour of Stone's is great, though, like every iteration of ginger you have ever had, from the thinly sliced stuff you get

with sushi, to candied root ginger, all the way to ginger nut biscuits. Along with the likes of Pimm's (which has a similar flavour) Stone's is one of the greatest names in dependable British aperitifs.

In a similar way to the Godfather (Scotch and amaretto) and the Rusty Nail (see pages 154–5), the Whisky Mac is kind of like a DIY Scotch whisky liqueur. The difference here being the innately wonderful marriage of ingredients that is ginger and Scotch. I say *innate*, but this is of course by design. That fragrant spice of ginger plays better with Scotch than any other ingredient I can think of. The trick is to pick the right kind of Scotch.

I would avoid any amount of peat characteristic and stick to a lighter style of malt or a blended whisky. Ideally, we should be mixing with a dram that is honeyed, but also full of green characteristics and perhaps some underlying spice. This will give the ginger wine something to latch on to: a palette of flavours for it to work with.

The finished effect should not be the taste of Scotch and ginger, but the taste of an entirely new drink. A drink that you just mixed and that will never be recreated in the same way again. It's in these drinks – the ones that were simply meant to be and are better than the sum of their parts – that we can identify what a great cocktail should be.

# BANANA BARREL WHISKY MAC

450 ML/15 FL. OZ. ABERFELDY 16-YEAR-OLD SCOTCH WHISKY
225 ML/7½ FL. OZ. BANANA BARREL GINGER WINE (*see below*)
50 G/1¾ OZ. SUGAR

Follow the recipe below and leave the mixture to rest for 3 months. It should now be ready to bottle. When I make ginger wine it's intended purely for Whisky Mac cocktails, so I bottle the wine with the whisky and store it pre-mixed.

It's worth mixing one up to check your preferred ratio, but I tend to bottle at 2:1 in favour of the whisky. My ginger wine recipe has little sweetness straight out of the barrel and is more acidic than shop-bought bottles, so you will definitely need

to sweeten it. If you store your Banana Barrel Whisky Mac in a dark cupboard it will keep indefinitely. I've found some of my older batches have improved over the years, as flavours meld together and the whisky and wine develop an affinity.

## BANANA BARREL GINGER WINE

Making your own ginger wine is super-easy and opens up loads of opportunities for customisation so that you can match your wine to your favourite whisky. Fermenting wines is also much more cost-effective than buying it off the shelf, and the bragging rights it will afford you are as good as it gets.

My recipe for ginger wine is intended for a long fermentation in a barrel, but you can do it in a winemaker's demijohn if you prefer. The beauty of using a barrel is that it will draw out some of those coconut and vanilla flavours that we associate with an oaked Chardonnay or bourbon whiskey. This will forge

a stronger relationship between the wine and whisky when you come to mix the cocktail.

To this end, I like to add a bit of sliced banana to my wine ferment, which forges a link between the fruit and the spice that drives the fermentation, and that barrel character will work its way into the liquid over time. The end product sits somewhere between a sweet sherry, bourbon whiskey, pot-still rum and good-quality ginger beer (yes, that delicious).

See page 53 for tips on buying barrels and pages 43–4 for further details on the fermentation process and technique.

150 G/5¼ OZ. GINGER ROOT (*no need to peel*)
700 G/1 LB. 9 OZ. SUGAR • 300 G/10½ OZ. HEATHER HONEY
20 G/¾ OZ. LEMON ZEST • 500 G/18 OZ. SULTANAS/GOLDEN RAISINS
7 G/¼ OZ. GRATED NUTMEG
300 G/10½ OZ PEELED AND SLICED BANANA (*roughly 3 bananas*)
5 LITRES/5¼ QUARTS WATER
120 ML/4 FL. OZ. LEMON JUICE (*roughly 4 lemons*)
7 G/¼ OZ. CHAMPAGNE YEAST
5 G/1 TEASPOON YEAST NUTRIENT

*Makes 5 litres/5¼ quarts*

Put the ginger root, the sugar, the honey, lemon zest, sultanas/golden raisins and nutmeg in a blender and blitz together until everything is powdered and begins to clump. Add the blended mixture to a 5-litre/5¼-quart sterilised plastic bucket and tip in 2.5 litres/2⅔ quarts of boiling water (you can use some of the water to rinse out the blender jug too). Chop the banana and boil in 500 ml/17 fl. oz. water for 20 minutes. Strain the banana water into the bucket. Add the remainder of the water and the lemon juice, and once the temperature drops below 25°C/77°F, add the yeast and the yeast nutrient and give it a really good stir with a sterilised whisk or spoon.

Cover the bucket loosely and stir once a day for 4 days. After 4 days, strain the liquid into a 10-litre/ 10½-quart barrel using a muslin/ cheesecloth and sterile funnel. Fit a bung and airlock valve to the top of the barrel and leave the contents to ferment in a warm place for a month.

Open the tap on the barrel and carefully strain out the liquid into a clean 5-litre/5¼-quart demijohn. The wine is ready for sweetening at this stage, but will clarify and improve with further resting.

# ❧ TEQUILA ❧

# EL DIABLO

½ A LARGE LIME
30 ML/1 FL. OZ. REPOSADO TEQUILA
15 ML/½ FL. OZ. CRÈME DE CASSIS
GINGER ALE

Squeeze the lime into the bottom of a small highball glass and drop the spent shell in there too. Add the tequila and the crème de cassis. Throw plenty of cubed ice in there and give it all a good stir. Top up nearly to the top with ginger ale (or ginger beer if you prefer) and add some more ice, followed by another quick stir. Garnish with a slice of lime.

There isn't a rule book to correctly initiate people into the world of tequila. Most of us are introduced to it either in the form of a shot (preceded by a lick of salt and closed out with a mouthful of lemon slice) or in a Margarita (see pages 190–2 of *The Curious Bartender*). The former of these two options usually takes place with a poor-quality *mixto* tequila, and the latter is invariably 'frozen' or just badly executed (and made with a *mixto* tequila). If, however, a rule book for tequila did exist, there would be no better drink to introduce people with than El Diablo.

Granted, the name (translating to 'the Devil') doesn't fill one with confidence of the potential pitfalls of this cocktail, but in truth it's not a particularly apt name and was probably chosen more for the drink's colour and general marketability than its effects. El Diablo is a long, refreshing cocktail that plays off two of tequila's boldest tasting notes: earthy piquancy and zingy fruit.

El Diablo is genetically little more than Buck or a Mule (see pages 98–100 of *The Curious Bartender*) or a Dark and Stormy (see pages 221–3 of *The Curious Bartender's Rum Revolution*), where the bitters have been replaced with crème de cassis and ginger ale selected over ginger beer. And it works a treat. That juicy blackcurrant is reminiscent of the fruitiness you get in a good Sangrita (see pages 195–6 of *The Curious Bartender*) and it softens the tequila while picking out some of its brighter qualities. Meanwhile, the ginger ale adds length, dryness and depth. El Diablo is one of those beverages that makes you salivate just thinking about it.

As far as the origins of this drink are concerned, it appears to have been invented by Trader Vic. Victor Bergeron is, of course, renowned as one of the pioneers of the tiki movement during the 1940s, which is best known for its liberal use of rum. But Vic's drinks weren't limited to cane-based intoxicants, and the occasional tequila, whisky and gin-spiked drink appears in Vic's sizeable body of work as well as on his cocktail menus.

The El Diablo made an entrance in Vic's first book, *Trader Vic's Book of Food and Drink* (1946). At that time its full name was Mexican El Diablo, which rather suggests that an earlier version of the cocktail once existed that did not use tequila as its base. By the late 1960s, Vic had dropped the 'Mexican'; in his 1968 *Pacific Island Cookbook*, it's simply El Diablo. Then, in a rather unusual turn of events, Vic published recipes for both a Mexican El Diablo and El Diablo in his revised *Trader Vic's Bartender's Guide* of 1972. The recipes are identical; only the construction of the cocktail (when exactly to add ice and the inclusion of a straw) differ.

# LOBELIA

40 ML / 1⅓ FL. OZ. DON JULIO BLANCO TEQUILA • 150 ML / 5 FL. OZ. RIBINGER FERMENT
*(see opposite)*

Add the tequila to a highball glass filled with ice and stir well. Carefully top up with the ferment, stirring as you go. I garnished with a blackcurrant leaf from my garden, but feel free to forgo the garnish altogether.

**Note:** Sometimes ferments do produce a small amount of alcohol too, which is something to be aware of if you're planning on serving them to children.

I'm lucky enough to own a few bars and I have a well-equipped drinks lab at my disposal. This means I can source all manner of ingredients and use a multitude of different techniques to get the best out of them, perfecting drinks concepts as I go. If I experiment long enough, I'm confident I can always find the best version of any ingredient and work out the most efficient way to extract its essence. As wonderful as that is, it sometimes means a recipe calls for highly specific products and specialist tech, which often takes the cocktail out of the realm of achievability for most high-end bars, let alone the amateur home bartender.

So this got me thinking: can you produce a truly original cocktail with nothing but common supermarket ingredients, a few bottles from your local off-licence and the most basic kitchen equipment? I'll admit it took me a few months before the answer hit me.

As is commonly the case, the best way forward is to look back. Many original cocktails were born out of kitchens rather than bars, and many of the best pieces of literature on bar craft from the early 20th century are in fact manuals for housewives that provided instruction on the best practices for manufacturing cordials, wines and ferments. Most often, these are simple recipes that are suitable for even the most basic kitchen environments. Most of them geared towards preservation of seasonal ingredients: pickling, curing, preserving and fermenting.

Fermentation has recently returned to some of the world's best bars as a method for creating super-complex ingredients at low cost from everyday fruit juices and syrups. The advantages of fermenting your own juices and cordials are legion: balanced sweetness and lactic acidity, natural fizz and documented health benefits.

I included two recipes with fermented components in *The Curious Bartender*: (Champagne Gin Fizz on pages 61–2 and Barrel Cart Mule on pages 99–100), but both drinks required a fair bit of prep work and about ten different ingredients.

Lobelia, named after a purple flower and almost an anagram of El Diablo, requires just three.

Ok, I lied. It requires five ingredients, but only if you include the water and the yeast. I consider yeast to be more of a tool than an ingredient, since it doesn't contribute flavour directly but, crucially, does *create* flavour while it's doing its thing. In any case, you will need to buy some yeast (baking aisle of supermarket).

The process is simple. Take store-bought blackcurrant cordial and ginger syrup, mix it with water and yeast, allow it to ferment for a few days, refrigerate, then mix with tequila to serve. The ferment should produce sufficient acidity to balance residual (unfermented) sugars in the cordial/syrup, but it'll also amalgamate the ginger and blackcurrant into a new union of taste and flavour that you will not believe possible from such rudimentary ingredients.

# RIBINGER FERMENT

100 ML / 3⅓ FL. OZ. GINGER SYRUP
*(Either from a bottle, or from a jar of preserved ginger)*
500 ML / 17 FL. OZ. ROUGHLY 25°C / 77°F WATER
3 G / ⅛ OZ. DRIED YEAST • 175–200 ML / 6–6¾ FL. OZ. RIBENA (BLACKCURRANT) CORDIAL

*Makes enough for 6 drinks*

Take a 1 litre/quart sterile plastic bottle and add to it 100 ml/3½ fl. oz. of the warm water and all of the yeast. Give the bottle a swirl and allow the yeast to hydrate for 5 minutes. Add the cordial, ginger syrup and the rest of the water, screw the cap on and give the liquid a good shake. Unscrew the cap, but leave it resting on top of the bottle. Let the bottle sit in a warm area for 2–3 days (shorter if it's really warm, longer if it's really cool).

Screw the cap on tightly and leave to rest for another day. Finally, put the bottle in the fridge. This stops the fermentation and is an essential stage if you wish to avoid a blackcurrant and ginger explosion. Where possible, allow the ferment to sit in the fridge for a few days, giving time for the yeast to settle at the bottom of the bottle. When you get around to opening the bottle, do so carefully to avoid the fizz disturbing the yeast.

# BATANGA

Coarse Sea Salt Flakes
60 ml/2 fl. oz. Don Julio Blanco Tequila
150 ml/5 fl. oz. Coca-Cola

Rim a highball glass with coarse sea salt flakes. Fill the glass with ice, then add the tequila and Coke. Give a good stir – preferably with a knife, as is Don Javier's preferred way – then squeeze a lime wedge on top.

Before we get into the details of this drink – for what there is of them – please allow me to own up to something. Until I started writing this book, I had only ever drunk eight Batangas, which were all consumed on one occasion, and in one particular bar. That bar is La Capilla, in the old part of the town of Tequila, Mexico.

Indeed, tequila gets its name from this town, which in the 19th century became renowned for the quality of the agave spirits it produced. La Capilla is the town's oldest surviving bar and the name translates as 'the Chapel'. Those on a pilgrimage to this hallowed hall will have a lot to be happy about. Not because La Capilla is a beautiful space, or because the drinks are out of this world, but because La Capilla is the distilled essence of what you wish every bar could be: comfortable, friendly, and imbued with the memory of a million drinks served, a million jokes cracked and a million spirits lifted.

The minister of ceremonies and distributor of communion at La Capilla is the original owner's grandson, Don Javier Delgado Corona, who is in his nineties. Don Javier is a living legend of the bar world, partly because of the warm welcome he offers everyone, but also because he invented two of the best tequila cocktails: the Paloma and the Batanga.

Unless you live in Mexico or work in a bar, you probably haven't ever mixed tequila and coke. But it's a winning combination; the spice and vegetal characteristics of the spirit are perfectly complemented by the citrus, nutmeg and cinnamon of the Coke. This mixture is a no-brainer in Mexico, where they consume more carbonated drinks per person than any other nation (half a litre per person per day). They drink a fair amount of tequila too.

To make a true Batanga, you ideally need to get hold of Mexican Coca-Cola. In Mexico, the Coke formula differs slightly from the rest of the world, because they make it with cane sugar instead of high-fructose corn syrup and the drink has about twice as much sodium in it.

The general consensus is that Mecican Coke tastes better, but it's been proven in studies that most people actually prefer the taste of the American version. The advantage of the Mexican product is down to perception and that it's served in glass bottles instead of plastic ones. In taste tests people prefer Coke served from glass. The flavour of the Mexican variety – and this may be my brain fooling me – does seem to take on a slightly more root beer-esque character reminiscent of lavender and aniseed. It also feels fizzier and more vibrant.

# COCA-QUILA

700 ML/24 FL. OZ. DON JULIO 1942 TEQUILA
30 G/1 OZ. SLICED ORANGE PEEL, PITH REMOVED
30 G/1 OZ. SLICED LEMON PEEL, PITH REMOVED
10 G/⅓ OZ. CRUSHED CINNAMON STICK
5 G/1 TEASPOON WHOLE CORIANDER SEEDS
1 WHOLE NUTMEG, CRUSHED
20 G/¾ OZ. COARSELY GROUND COFFEE
150 G/5¼ OZ. SUGAR • 3 G/⅛ OZ. SALT
5 ML/1 TEASPOON ORANGE FLOWER WATER

Take a large mason jar or plastic container and add to it the tequila, the citrus peels, cinnamon, coriander seeds, nutmeg and coffee. Seal the jar/container and store in a warm place for 2–4 weeks, or until you're happy that the flavours have been extracted. Strain the liquid through a muslin/cheesecloth, then mix with the sugar, salt and orange flower water.

Unlike vodka, rum and bourbon, agave spirits have mostly avoided the indignity of being sold as 'flavoured' products. Perhaps this is because flavoured spirits usually target younger drinkers and tequila already has that demographic all sewn up. Or perhaps it's because agave spirits are packed with flavour already and simply do not need help from ancillary ingredients. Or maybe it's that tequila doesn't pair well with other flavours? I'll be honest and say that I've only ever tasted one flavoured tequila product, Patrón XO Cafe, which is infused with coffee and is actually rather nice. There are a small number of other flavoured tequilas on the market, however, all of which (rose, strawberry, salted caramel…) sound like abominations.

So the questions is, are we all missing a trick here, and is it possible to make a delicious-tasting flavoured spirit with tequila or mescal as a base? The answer is: yes.

And what better flavour to imbue into a bottle of tequila than one of the most popular flavours in all of Mexico: Coke.

The recipe for Coke is not as much of a secret as Coca-Cola might have you believe. Of course, the exact proportions are known only to Coca-Cola, but the ingredients are common knowledge. Besides the obvious water, sugar, caramel colouring, caffeine and

phosphoric acid, which are all listed as ingredients on the bottle, there are a collection of other flavours that mix together to form the Coke taste that are not on the label. Those flavours are: orange oil, cinnamon oil, lemon oil, coriander seed oil, nutmeg oil and neroli (orange flower) oil. Some readers might remember that I used these ingredients in their natural forms to create a homemade cola for my CL 1901 cocktail in *The Curious Bartender*, which was based on an earlier recipe for homemade cola that I developed in 2009.

For my Coca-Quila, I will infuse the same natural ingredients into a bottle of tequila. To quote an old Pepsi advertising slogan, it'll be a, 'Taste That Beats the Others Cold'.

This recipe approaches infusions the old-fashioned way, through the cold steeping of fruits and spices into the liquid for a couple of weeks. This is good, because it means you don't need any equipment besides a knife, chopping board and a set of scales.

I suggest that you sweeten the tequila, which will amplify the flavours of the fruit peels and spices, as well as that of the inherent agave character. I add a touch of salt to mine too, to replicate that flavour of Mexican Coke and also to pay homage to Don Javier's legendary Batanga.

# TEQUILA SUNRISE

40 ML/1⅓ FL. OZ. OCHO BLANCO TEQUILA
120 ML/4 FL. OZ. CHILLED, PRESSED AND FILTERED ORANGE JUICE
15 ML/½ FL. OZ. GRENADINE

Add the tequila and orange juice to a mixing glass and stir over ice for a minute. Strain into a small, chilled highball glass. Pour the grenadine over the top.

Modern speakeasies have done a good job of romanticising the Prohibition period, when the sale and supply of alcohol became illegal in the US. But it's a common misconception that illegal drinking dens in New York and Washington were filled with well-dressed patrons, sipping on perfectly concocted Martinis and Manhattans. The reality was poor-quality or counterfeit booze mixed by B-team bartenders who were left behind after all the real talent disappeared off to Europe. Of course, outside of the US, it was still possible to get a decent drink, and there were a handful of enduring classics that were invented during this time. Most of these drinks were formulated by American bartenders working in London and Paris. But there was at least one classic cocktail created during this time in North America, just across the US/Mexico border, in Tijuana.

If you found yourself on the west coast of the States and in need of a fix during the 1920s, you might have visited Tijuana's Agua Caliente tourist complex, which consisted of a casino, hotel, golf course and racetrack, and even had its own airstrip. If you did, it's possible you'd have bumped into Charlie Chaplin, Rita Hayworth, or Laurel and Hardy. Agua Caliente's close proximity to the US border made it an attractive solution to a big problem. It's in this resort that the words 'tequila' and 'sunrise' were put together for the first time. That's not to say the drink was invented there, but *a drink* was invented there that went by the same name.

First appearing in writing in *Bottoms Up! Y Como!*, a drinking brochure published by Agua Caliente resort in 1933, the 'Sunrise tequila' comprised a refreshing-sounding mixture of tequila, lime, grenadine, crème de cassis and soda water – so rather more like an El Diablo (see page 172) than the Tequila Sunrise as we know it today.

While a version of the Tequila Sunrise may have enjoyed popularity during Prohibition, the drink failed to penetrate America immediately following its repeal. A 1941 advert for Caesar's Hotel (of salad fame) in Tijuana advertised a Tequila Sunrise, but the drink rarely featured on any drinks lists through the 1950s. By the 1960s the cocktail had mostly evolved into a kind of tequila sour, sweetened with grenadine, and it was only in the 1970s that orange juice began to feature. Having shed most its redeeming features, the Tequila Sunrise shot to global fame.

This widespread adoption and adulteration of the Sunrise was partly down to the growing interest in tequila in general. Tequila was the wild and racy alternative to vodka's mediocrity. Vodka drinkers wore grey flannel suits while tequila drinkers wore nothing at all. Both dangerous and delicious, tequila afforded those who dared to drink it a kind of worldly aura. The Margarita was the flag bearer for this movement, but the Tequila Sunrise led the cavalry charge.

So what does it taste like? Well, unsurprisingly, this depends on the quality of your orange juice and your tequila. I recommend using a 100 per cent agave blanco in this instance, as woody notes don't pair well with the brightness of the OJ. Freshly pressed is the way to go with the orange, but be sure to filter out the pulp. I've found that off-the-shelf grenadine works just fine. My final tip is to ensure that the drink is as cold as humanly possible. This will take the edge off the syrup's sweetness and remove any danger of flabbiness and citrus fatigue.

# TEQUILA SOLERO

My main gripe with the Tequila Sunrise is how sweet and sticky it is. Orange juice is packed full of sugar, and grenadine, well… grenadine is *sweet*. Normally bartenders counteract sweetness by adding citrus, but there's plenty of acidity in this drink already and more acid will seriously impact the biology of your stomach and turn your tongue furry. The next best solution to dialling down the sweetness is to make the drink colder.

The colder you make a drink, the more it suppresses our perception of its sweetness. This is why ice cream tastes surprisingly sweet once it melts. It's also why popsicles/ice pops turn into syrup when you try and drink them after they've melted. So if we treat a Tequila Sunrise like a melted popsicle/ice pop, the solution to this problem appears: freeze the drink into an ice lolly.

Of course, all the best frozen lollies are not just delicious to eat, but also incredible to look at. From the twisted architecture of the Twister to the layered colours of the Rocket Lolly, visual appeal is just as important, if not more so, than the flavour. The Tequila Sunrise already has visual appeal with that graduation from glacé cherry-red all the way to mellow yellow. But a true Sunrise also has lots of blue and purple in it, as the night sky is pushed further west. So I'm going to layer my frozen cocktail all the way from red though to deep purple.

To achieve this I will need to layer each colour on top of one another prior to freezing. This opens up new possibilities with regard to the tequila (or mezcal) I use, as each new layer has the option to feature a different spirit that pairs with the respective fruit flavours. For the red base of the lolly I'm going to use pomegranate, chilli and *añejo* tequila. The central, yellow layer will be orange juice, juiced yellow pepper and mezcal. And the top, purple layer will be *blanco* tequila with blackcurrant, lime and ginger. The trick with layering is to always place the sweeter, low-alcohol ingredients on the bottom, and float the dryer, boozy ingredients on the top.

Like a journey through classic Mexican cocktails, this frozen treat will combine elements of the Tequila Sunrise, Sangrita and El Diablo… the perfect *compañero* for a day by the pool.

## PURPLE LAYER

60 ml/2 fl. oz. Crème de Cassis
60 ml/2 fl. oz. Lime Juice
60 ml/2 fl. oz. Don Julio Blanco Tequila
20 ml/⅔ fl. oz. Ginger Syrup
40 ml/1⅓ fl. oz. Water

## YELLOW LAYER

220 ml/7½ fl. oz. Filtered Orange Juice
110 ml/3¾ fl. oz. Juiced Yellow (Bell) Pepper
*(requires a blender or juicer)*
20 g/¾ oz. Sugar
70 ml/2⅓ fl. oz. Santo Di Pedra Mezcal

## RED LAYER

100 ml/3½ fl. oz. Pomegranate Juice
20 ml/⅔ fl. oz. Lime Juice
20 ml/⅔ fl. oz. Grenadine
100 ml/3½ fl. oz. Don Julio Añejo Tequila
Chilli Sauce

*Makes 6 x 150-g/5¼-oz. ice lollies/popsicles*

You'll need 6 x 150-g/5¼-oz. lolly moulds for this.

Mix the ingredients for each layer and keep them in mixing beakers or small jugs/pitchers. Next, set up your lolly mould and pour 70 ml/ 2⅓ fl. oz. of the yellow layer into the base of each mould. Then tilt your moulds towards you slightly, and pour 40 ml/1⅓ fl. oz. of the purple layer steadily down the side of each mould. Being sweeter, the purple liquid should sink to the bottom.

Finally, using a teaspoon or the base of a bar spoon, carefully float 40 ml/1⅓ fl. oz. of the red layer on top of the yellow. Adjust your freezer to its lowest possible temperature and place the moulds in the bottom and freeze for a minimum of 6 hours. If your freezer is too warm, it may struggle to freeze boozy liquids such as this.

Once the lollies are fully set, pour a little cold water over the outside of the moulds and carefully slip the frozen lolly out. Return the lolly to the freezer for 30 minutes, or until you're ready to enjoy them.

# WINE

# CHAMPAGNE COCKTAIL

2 DASHES PEYCHAUD'S BITTERS • I SMALL BROWN SUGAR LUMP
120 ML/4 FL. OZ. CHILLED CHAMPAGNE

Dash the bitters onto the sugar cube, then drop the cube into a chilled Champagne flute. Carefully pour the Champagne down the inside edge of the flute, being careful not to pour too fast, so as to avoid frothing. Pour right to the top, then finish with a twist of lemon (which you can discard).

According to the definition from the newspaper *The Balance and Columbian Repository* (1806), a cocktail is 'spirits of any kind, sugar, water, and bitters'. So if you mix bourbon with sugar, water and bitters, you have a Whiskey Cocktail. If you mix brandy with sugar, water and bitters… Ok, you get it. But what about if you mix Champagne with sugar, water and bitters? Well, then you have a slightly sweet, slightly bitter, and very much overly diluted glass of Champagne. But if we treat the Champagne as a mixture of spirit and water (which is exactly what it is, if you think about it), then we need only add bitters and sugar. Then you have something delicious. Then you have a Champagne Cocktail.

The Champagne Cocktail was born during the early days of cocktail bartending. The first written reference to the drink comes from Robert Tomes' 1855 book about Panama, which detailed such matters as the economy, culture and drinking establishments of the central American isthmus during the construction of the Panama Railway.

Tomes wrote, 'I profess the belief that drinking Champagne cock–tails[sic] before breakfast, and smoking forty cigars daily, to be an immoderate enjoyment of the good things of this world.'

I think most doctors would agree. Tomes goes on to recount how the drink is constructed using 'sparkling "Mumm"… a dropping of bitters… pounded crystal ice, pattered in to tumblers…[and] sugar'.

Two things about Tomes's instructions are interesting. The first is that the drink is served over crushed ice in a tumbler. The use of ice places the drink that little bit closer to being a true cocktail, seeing as water is a cocktail ingredient, and it means the drink would probably be colder than the modern version, but hey, they were in Panama, for pity's sake. The second interesting thing is that no brandy or Cognac is called for in the recipe, as is customary these days.

In turns out that most classic cocktail books agree that brandy has no place in this drink, whether it's *Jerry Thomas' Bar-Tender's Guide* (1862) or Harry Craddock's *The Savoy Cocktail Book* (1930). The first book to include brandy in the Champagne Cocktail, as far as I can tell, is W. J. Tarling's *Café Royal Cocktail Book* (1937), where the instruction is to use 'a dash of brandy as required'.

A modern recipe would generally call for 25 ml/¾ fl. oz. of Cognac to be topped up with Champagne. That means the alcohol content of the average Champagne Cocktail has doubled from about 8% ABV in the 1850s (accounting for dilution from the ice) to 16% today.

But for patrons happy to splash at least £15/$21 on a drink, it's not the strength of the Champagne Cocktail that gets them anxious, but the sweetness. That sugar cube fizzing away is like a time bomb to the Champagne connoisseur, who craves dryness from the drink. But it's important to recognise that the sugar in this drink will not contribute much in the way of detectable sweetness. The main purpose of the sugar is to create bubbles, and the rough surface of a sugar cube couldn't be better designed for bubble manufacture. The $CO_2$ in the Champagne positively gushes out of the drink as thousands of bubbles form.

This cocktail is fantastic visual theatre and prompts nearby guests to order one themselves. But getting back to what I was saying, the freezing Champagne is pretty bad at dissolving the hard sugar lump, so it tends to only be the last couple of sips that contain any sweetness.

# LIAR'S CHAMPAGNE

700 ML/24 FL. OZ. Chablis • 50 ML/1⅔ FL. OZ. Dry Amontillado Sherry
25 ML/¾ FL. OZ. Bols Genever • 5 ML/1 teaspoon Green Chartreuse

Mix the ingredients together, chill, and then carbonate using your preferred method (see pages 55–9). In this instance I would (for once) recommend using a soda syphon, because it's nice to serve the drink as a sharing cocktail in an ice bucket. Follow the instructions on page 58 and be sure to vent and carbonate at least two times. Real vintage Champagnes tend to be less fizzy than younger Champagnes, so if you're aiming for a true representation you won't need crazy levels of fizz in your drink.

I consider Champagne an overrated drink. It's not that I don't like it, it's just that if I have £25/$35 to spend in a wine shop I know it'll go a hell of a lot further on a great bottle of Bordeaux or Burgundy. And that's because Champagne is a massively overpriced fizzy white wine. Almost all of the perceived value comes not from the liquid but from the archaic reputation of the name and its association with extravagance and celebration.

That said, I'm always happy to be proven wrong, and I've tasted some vintage Champagnes and prestige cuvées in the past that have been outstanding. However, many of those bottles cost four figures (I wasn't paying) so are hugely impractical as everyday drinks and generally out of most folks' budgets even on the most special of special occasions. And let's face it, no drink on the planet is worthy of a £1,000/$1,400 price tag through liquid credentials alone, so you're still paying a premium for the rarity of the bottle and the bragging rights of getting to drink it.

To put it in simple terms: all Champagne is overpriced, but only the really overpriced bottles taste any good. Wouldn't it be great then, if we could make something taste like 'very good' Champagne for less money than it costs to buy a cheap Champagne?

The best Champagnes I have tasted have tended to be blanc de blancs (made from the Chardonnay grape) and aged for a minimum of ten years in the bottle. This long period (for a wine) in glass allows the liquid to uncoil and resolve itself into something deeper and more complex. Simulating this effect is no mean feat.

Step one is to understand what a great Champagne tastes like and how it differs from a cheaper wine. To identify the taste and aroma of these expensive wines, I originally planned to spend thousands on some nice bottles and had a rather lovely party. My wife talked me out of it though (I'll never forgive her), so instead I decided to just ask a sommelier what it is that defines a great vintage. But then it occurred to me – why ask one sommelier when you can ask *all of them?*

To do this, I called upon the vast knowledge-base known as the internet. Online wine communities publish thousands of tasting notes, and they freely gave me the data I needed to find shared features of the very best vintage Champagnes. I split each tasting note into individual words and number of occurrences, and I found useable taste and flavour descriptors, starting with 'toasty' and 'savoury' and then 'fresh', 'full', 'rich', 'lemon', 'tight', 'herbal', 'bready' and 'yeasty'. Using these flavour descriptors as a target taste profile, I was in a position to make my Liar's Champagne.

For the wine base I used a white Burgundy, made from 100 per cent Chardonnay grapes. Specifically, I went for an unoaked Chablis that provides the fresh and lemony base to my wine. You should be able to pick up a Chablis for under £10/$14. To get the toast and bread notes, I wanted to fortify the wine with a touch of genever, which tastes like just that: toast and bread. More toast, along with savoury richness, tightness and yeastiness will come from a seasoning of amontillado sherry. The herbal note will come from a tiny lick of Chartreuse.

# SHERRY COBBLER

60 ML/2 FL. OZ. DRY OLOROSO SHERRY • 15 ML/½ FL. OZ. SUGAR SYRUP (*see page 32*)
15 ML/½ FL. OZ. FRESH GRAPEFRUIT JUICE
(*you can use apple, orange or pineapple if you prefer*)
6 FRESH RASPBERRIES OR BLACKBERRIES

Fill a tumbler or rocks glass with crushed ice and add all of the ingredients. Give it a good stir and
top up with more crushed ice. Garnish with a sprig of mint and serve with a paper straw.

Cobblers are an old family of cocktails from the Iron Age of American bartending and were originally made from a base of wine mixed with fruit, sugar and some citrus. A sort of single-serve punch, if you will. Any wine will do, but sherry is king here. That nutty character of a good oloroso turns into pure addiction when paired with fresh fruit, ice and little sweetness. It's madness that these drinks don't feature on more cocktail menus, particularly since they are relatively cheap to produce and super-simple to bash together.

Now, if it were only this drink's deliciousness that made it special, I would probably rest my case right here. But there's a lot more to the history and influence of the of the cobbler than appears at first glance.

The first cobblers came about in America in the early 19th century, some time between 1810 and 1830, roughly coinciding with the invention of the Mint Julep, of which it is a close relation. In fact, the first written reference to the cobbler was in 1838, the same year that the first Mint Julep was served at the Kentucky Derby. Just like the julep, cobblers are traditionally made with crushed ice. This approach gets things cold nice and quickly, and it means you can do away with shaking and just build in the glass if it pleases you.

Crushed ice in a cocktail presents one or two issues, however, such as when you go to tip the glass up and the ice cascades down on your face. The issue is compounded when you have fresh fruit mixed in there too (as you do with a cobbler), which tumbles down your cheeks like large fruity tears. The Mint Julep got around this issue with the julep strainer – a kind of sieve that sat on top of the serving vessel (now used by many bartenders to strain stirred cocktails) – and early cobblers were served in this manner too. A neater solution would, of course, have been a drinking straw. Only problem was they hadn't been invented then.

Well, that's not strictly true. The first known pictogram of alcohol consumption, which comes from ancient Sumeria, shows revellers drinking through straws shoved into a large pot of beer. During the 1800s, straws made from rye grass became popular, but they had a tendency to dissolve into mush. Metal straws and straws made from tubular pasta (yes, really) also existed, but commercially produced straws didn't arrive until the 1880s. Marvin Stone's patent for the first paper drinking straw was made from rolled-up paper coated in wax. If you were a cobbler drinker – and given that it was one of the most popular cocktails in America during the 1880s, you probably were – the drinking straw would be the greatest marvel until sliced bread was invented some 40 years later.

Some bartenders preferred to shake their cobblers, however, and that's the method that Jerry Thomas instructed in his *Bar-Tender's Guide* (1862). At that time, the cobbler was one of the only cocktails that you would have bothered to shake. Not least because the cocktail shaker didn't exist until 1872, when a patent was filed by William Harnett of Brooklyn for his 'apparatus for mixed drinks'. Harnett's shaker was painfully overengineered, though, consisting of six covered tumblers mounted on a plunger-based system. Twelve years later, Edward Hauck, also of Brooklyn, patented the three-piece shaker that we know and love – the shaker that became widely known as the cobbler shaker.

# BLENDED SHERRY SLUSHY

700 ML/24 FL. OZ. TIO PEPE FINO SHERRY • 60 ML/2 FL. OZ. PX SHERRY
100 ML/3½ FL. OZ. POMEGRANATE JUICE • 10 ML/⅓ FL. OZ. ROSEWATER

Freeze all of the sherry in ice-cube moulds (or in a plastic container – you can break the
block apart once it's frozen). Add the frozen sherry and all of the other ingredients to a
blender and blitz on full speed until it forms a cohesive, slushy texture. Serve immediately,
garnishing with a twist of lemon.

Sherry is a drink that is very close to my heart and extremely close to my stomach (because more often than not it is in my stomach). This is partly because I co-own a sherry bar in London called Sack, named after the former British term for the *seco* (dry) wines of southern Spain, and partly because sherry is so damn delicious… which is why I own a sherry bar (it's a chicken and egg kind of thing). Being both fortified and aged in cask, sherry is that little bit closer to being a spirit than any other wine. Couple that with its long-standing relationship with the Scotch whisky industry, and you have a liquid that ought to be of special interest to anyone who calls themselves a bartender.

So why don't we drink more sherry? Well, we did. Once upon a time, wines from the Spanish sherry-producing region centred around the town of Jerez de la Frontera were held in as high a regard as any French wine-producing region. But the latter part of the 20th century was brutally unkind to sherry, as consumer demands favoured sweeter and cheaper blends, distorting both the flavour and the reputation of the category.

Fortunately, we're now in the midst of a growing trend towards real sherry. But it still needs a little bit of a helping hand if it's to make itself cool once again. And just because it tastes great on its own, it doesn't mean you can't mix great drinks with it. Great drinks such as my Sherry Slushy.

Before we get into that, though, let's talk about temperature. Different styles of sherry should be served at different temperatures and it's typically the older and non-biologically aged ones (oloroso) that prefer to be a little warmer. Super-dry wines that are aged under *flor*

(yeast), like fino and manzanilla, should be as cold as possible, however. Super-chilling these wines highlights the skeletal structure of them, amplifying salinity and helping the liquid slip down at an alarming rate.

We installed a slushy machine in Sack about a year after the bar opened. I'm aware that these machines don't generally speak of careful flavour balance and high-provenance liquid, but that was the idea, challenging preconceptions of a stuffy drinks category by serving the drink in the least stuffy possible manner.

The Sherry Slushy is more of a concept than a recipe that requires strict adherence. The only rules are that you have to use a fino sherry and some fruit or herbal modifiers. With the latter I avoid citrus as it's too sour, so consider fruits such as pomegranate, raspberry, strawberry, blackcurrant and cranberry. The berry flavours pair well with the Palomino grape character in the wine.

If you want to beef the drink up a little, throw a dash of spirit in there too – I find that gin, agricole rum and blanco tequila all work well – but for me this is a session cocktail, which should be kept at a relatively low ABV. I've also chosen to use a Pedro Ximenez sherry (a sweet style of sherry with bags of dried-fruit character), so you don't need to add sugar.

Now, I realise most bars and households don't have a slushy machine, so the recipe above is intended for a blender. The downside of using a blender is that it does require some prep work though, since normal (water) ice will overly dilute your drink. The solution? Make sherry ice of course!

# SANGRIA

750 ML/25 FL. OZ. TEMPRANILLO WINE
100 ML/3½ FL. OZ. RASPBERRY GIN
150 ML/5 FL. OZ. FRESH LEMON JUICE
75 ML/2½ FL. OZ. SUGAR SYRUP (*see page 32*)

Add all of the ingredients to a large pitcher and stir with plenty of ice.
Garnish with slices of citrus fruit.

Sangria is one of those drinks that only works in the right time and place. The kind of drink you wouldn't dream of ordering unless you're sitting by a pool in Spain, but handily provides most of your daily calorific intake when you are. Lots of drinks evoke a sense of place regardless of where you are when you choose to enjoy them. Other drinks really do require you to be *in that place* to appreciate them properly. Sangria falls into the latter camp. It is the liquid embodiment of lazy (and hazy) afternoons with friends, seasoned with salty morsels of tapas and the nagging feeling that wine will never taste this good ever again.

Sangria is basically a type of punch made from a base of red wine and brandy or rum. You find many drinks like this outside of the Iberian peninsular, but you'd be incorrect in thinking it has always been this way. Wine punches have been enjoyed in Europe since the 17th century and have their roots in the Hippocratic wines (or *hippocras*) that emerged out of Dark Ages Europe in the 15th century, around the same time as *aqua vitae* first arrived.

It was a simple trick: you take poor-quality wine and add to it herbs, spices, fruits, sugar, or just more booze, and what you're left with tastes better than what you started with, and it gets you drunk quicker (an essential feature of any 15th-century beverage).

While some took to doctoring low-quality plonk in efforts to emulate the wines of the great chateaux of France (see pamphlets on the subject, such as *A New and Easie Way to Make Twenty-Three Sorts of Wine, Equal to That of France* from 1701 and John Yarworth's *New Treatise on Artificial Wines* from 1690), others dedicated

their time to creating elaborate punches with wine at the heart.

The wines in question were varied, from port to Riesling and everything in between. Punch Royal consisted of Rhenish wine with lemon juice, ginger, cinnamon, nutmeg, brandy, musk and ambergris (a deeply aromatic, waxy substance produced in the digestive system of a sperm whale, no less). Ruby Punch, which appears in *Oxford Nightcaps* (1827) was a combination of port, lemon juice, rum and tea.

Of course if you live in Spain, you've little use for warming winter spices, so they get substituted for more fruit and perhaps some fresh herbs, and what you're left with is Sangria. There's no known date for the invention of Sangria (the name is thought to come from the Spanish word 'sangue', meaning 'blood'), and it seems likely that it simply evolved organically from the wider European trend of wine punches. One day it wasn't there, the next day it was, and nobody seemed to notice anything had changed.

And because we have no inventor to credit, there's no *de facto* recipe for Sangria. Red wine is a must, then there's citrus juice, some sugar, some brandy or other spirit, then add whatever other fruits and herbs fit your personal preferences.

In my recipe I like to amplify the red-fruit flavours of Spanish Tempranillo wine (the grape used to make Rioja) by fortifying it with a raspberry-infused gin. I then use purely lemon juice (no orange), along with sugar and ice. You can easily infuse fresh raspberries into a bottle of gin (leave in a warm place for a week) or buy one of the many brands producing raspberry gin.

# CLARET

60 ml/2 fl. oz. LBV Port • 20 ml/⅔ fl. oz. Blood Orange Juice
5 ml/1 teaspoon Citric Acid Solution (see page 35)
10 ml/⅓ fl. oz. Clove & Woodruff Syrup (see opposite)
15 ml/½ fl. oz. Blood (see page 4)

Add all of the ingredients to a cocktail shaker filled with ice. Shake well for 10 seconds, strain the drink and throw the ice away. Shake again without ice for 10 seconds. Pour into a chilled Nick & Nora glass.

I'm just going to come straight out with it: this cocktail contains blood. Yes, this might be a bit of a gimmick. Yes, it does sound a little off-putting. But bear with me.

There are cultures all over the world that consume blood, from Mexican blood omelettes to Vietnamese blood-drinking rituals. Despite the prevalence of black pudding in the UK, Ireland and parts of Europe, we have developed a greater aversion to it than other parts of the world. I'll admit there is something uncomfortably primal about sipping on the literal lifeblood of another creature. It goes without saying that any drink containing blood is not suitable for vegetarians, but for all you carnivores out there who are unsure, let me ask you this: if you're going to eat meat, why not eat the whole animal?

One of the amazing things about blood is that it has a high albumin protein content. Albumin is the same protein that we find in egg whites, which allows us to make mousses, meringues and, of course, sour cocktails that normally call for a foamy head. Both egg white and blood have roughly the same protein content level, so you can easily switch out egg for blood in pretty much any recipe. It also means that blood is good for foaming and emulsification.

But there's more: in blood we find the protein *serum albumin* and in eggs it's *ova albumin*. It's estimated that up to 2.5 per cent of Europeans have albumin intolerance, but it's an intolerance against *ova albumin*, not the albumin found in blood. If you have an egg intolerance and have been dying to enjoy the delicate texture of a true sour cocktail, blood may be your best option!

In this sour-style cocktail, I can replace the usual egg-white component with blood, giving me all the foam that I would expect to see in any other sour, and a deep scarlet hue. The only problem then is the haemoglobin in the blood, which is the part that gives that sharp, metallic and, to put it frankly, horrible taste. Therefore, the rest of the ingredients in the cocktail will work in concert to mellow out that taste.

As tempting as it is to use claret in this drink, I'm going to match my blood (well, the blood of a French pig, actually) with a nice LBV port. The port will bring in some rich tobacco notes as well as plenty of dry, dark, fruit characteristics.

For the citrus component, it has to be blood orange juice – for its name, its colour and most of all for its wonderful tartness. Now, you could simply sweeten this drink with sugar syrup, but I've opted to use a syrup made from cloves and the fragrant herb called woodruff. When the Nordic Food Lab spent three months testing various bloody recipes back in 2013, clove and woodruff were picked out as two of the better flavour matches.

But it's not just the blood that works here. Clove pairs brilliantly with orange (think festive Buck's Fizz), but it'll also amplify leather and grape characteristics in the port too. Woodruff, on the other hand, is traditionally used in the manufacture of the German equivalent of Sangria – May Wine. This drink is made from woodruff and a base of German white wine, along with sugar, brandy and fresh fruit. So you can see that there is a natural synergy between all of these ingredients, and it's the blood that truly binds them.

# CLOVE & WOODRUFF SYRUP

500 ML/17 FL. OZ. WATER
500 G/1 LB. 2 OZ. SUGAR
20 G/¾ OZ. DRIED WOODRUFF LEAVES *or* 120 G/4¼ OZ. FRESH WOODRUFF
10 G/⅓ OZ. WHOLE CLOVES

Combine all of the ingredients together in a vacuum pouch/ziplock bag and place in
a water bath set to 55°C/131°F for 4 hours. Strain the contents through a muslin/
cheesecloth while still hot. Store in the fridge for up to a month.

# AMERICANO

25 ml/¾ fl. oz. Campari
25 ml/¾ fl. oz. Cocchi Vermouth di Torino • 75 ml/2½ fl. oz. Soda Water

Add the Campari and vermouth to a chilled highball filled with cubes of ice. Stir well for a minute
then top up with soda as desired (I recommend 75–100 ml/2½–3½ fl. oz.) and stir again briefly.
Garnish with a wedge of orange.

The richness and diversity of Italian food and drink culture can in part be attributed to the fact that, up until the 1860s, Italy was an assemblage of warring states. Every region had its own cuisine and drinking rituals, and the manufacture of products was extremely small-scale artisanal in nature. This began to change after the formation of the kingdom of Italy in 1861, when production ramped up and newly commercialised products became available across the land.

One such item was vermouth. For around 100 years vermouth production had centred around the town of Turin, the capital of the former kingdom of Savoy. This slightly fortified, slightly bitter, slightly herbaceous wine had arrived from Germany in the middle of the 18th century, where it was known as *Wermut* (after wormwood, the bitter herb that seasons the drink).

As the north of Italy industrialised rapidly, Italian vermouth hit US shores only a few years after Italian unification. Brands such as Martini Sola & Cia, Carpano and Cora leveraged the romance of Italian culture to the American market, and the drink quickly became the darling of the new cocktail revolution. Mixed only with bitters, it featured on the menu at Delmonico's restaurant in New York as the Vermouth Cocktail in 1868. But as time went by, it would be as a supporting role that vermouth would leave its lasting mark in American cocktail history.

Meanwhile, Italian booze makers got wind of these so-called cocktails and thought they might have a go. The vermouth part wasn't a problem, so now to just find some bitters. Well, it turns out that pharmacists and monks had been making *amaro* (Italian for 'bitter')

intended for medicinal purposes for centuries, but it was only in the industrial era that the world saw the arrival of familiar brand names like Averna, Campari, Fernet-Branca and Ramazzotti.

Unlike American bitters, which were effectively a 'seasoning', Italian bitters were drinks in their own right that tended to be less bitter and a lot sweeter. Pairing bitter *amaro* with Italian vermouth to create an American-style cocktail wouldn't have taken a great deal of imagination. And thus, the Americano was born.

The earliest examples of the Americano came in bottle form, manufactured by industrious vermouth and *amaro* producers, who even went as far as to place American flags on their labels. Later, in the early 20th century, customisation of this basic formula ensued as folk became particular about which vermouth or *amaro* filled their glass, and whether ice or soda was added to the mix. All this experimental mixology culminated in the invention of the Negroni in 1919, where gin jostled its way into the mixture.

With all these variations flying around, it's better to view the Americano as a concept rather than a rigid formula. Contemporary recipes see equal parts Italian vermouth and *amaro* served long, with ice and soda water. And when you look at the primary function of today's Americano – an aperitif – this makes perfect sense.

Vermouth and *amaro* are too sweet for pre-dinner drinking, but chilling, diluting and carbonating them tackles the sweetness head-on. Thankfully the bitterness of the *amaro* is tenacious enough to survive some watering down and after it all what you're left with is something, well… something perfect.

# AMERICANO IN BOTTIGLIA

150 ML/5 FL. OZ. CAMPARI • 150 ML/5 FL. OZ. COCCHI VERMOUTH DI TORINO
200 ML/6¾ FL. OZ. COLD AEROPRESS COFFEE • 400 ML/13½ FL. OZ. MINERAL WATER

*Makes 6 x 150-ml/5-fl. oz. bottles*

Mix the ingredients together in large bottles and put them in the freezer until the liquid is on the verge of freezing. Chill your bottles at the same time. Once it's as cold as can be, pour the liquid into each bottle and carbonate individually (see pages 55–9). Store the sealed bottles in the fridge and enjoy straight from the bottle or in a chilled highball glass. No ice needed.

I'm a big lover of bottled cocktails, particularly when they are carbonated – there's something special about a little single-serve package that contains lots of flavour and lots of bubbles. Highball drinks that call for carbonated ingredients count as some of my favourite cocktails, but I can't help but wish they were a little fizzier at times. The problem is, when mixing spirits and liqueurs with soda water, you are also mixing non-carbonated ingredients with carbonated and diluting the fizz. Bottling and carbonating *all* of the ingredients of the cocktail overcomes this problem.

As clever as that might be, carbonating three off-the-shelf ingredients is hardly the epitome of modern mixology. So to keep things interesting, I'm going to add a subtle twist to my Americano cocktail. Can you guess what it is? – An *americano*.

If you've ever ordered an Americano (cocktail) in a bar outside Italy, there's a good chance you had to follow up your order with, 'The cocktail, not the coffee.' The coffee drink (which comprises espresso and hot water) got its name under similar circumstances to the cocktail. American troops serving in Italy during World War II found the Italian espresso to be too strong for their tastes. They asked for it to be diluted with water to mimic the filter coffee that they were used to at home. The Italians thought this practice was most amusing ('*acqua al nostro espresso?!*') and named the drink 'Americano'.

I'm not a fan of Americanos, and I view them as a botched workaround to a delicious, long cup of black coffee. Espresso is a very particular way of brewing strong coffee that performs well as a short shot with

dark roasted and blended coffee. Add water to it and you lose a lot of that magic. Black filter coffee, on the other hand, is designed to be brewed long, from single-origin coffee, and is typically roasted lighter, so tends to make a better 'cup of joe' – a term that we can also thank the American military for.

Combining americano and Americano isn't just for novelty value, I hasten to add. The first steam-driven espresso machine was invented by Angelo Moriondo in the 1880s and presented at the Turin General Exposition in 1884. Later designs that paved the way for modern machines came from brands like Pavoni, Gaggia and Faema, all of which were based in Milan. Just like the components of the Americano (cocktail), espresso coffee was born out of these two progressive cities.

For my Americano in Bottiglia, I'm going to use an Aeropress to hot-brew my coffee, then chill it down and mix it with Campari and vermouth prior to carbonation. You could use cold-brew coffee for this, but cold brew tends to lack acidity, which is something I feel will benefit this drink in bringing out the winey notes of the vermouth. For the carbonation stage you can use a sodastream, iSi whipper, or a full-on carbonation rig (see pages 56–8) set to 42 PSI. For the Aeropress coffee (other paper-filter brew methods will work too), you'll need 16 g of light roasted coffee and 240 g nearly boiling water. Coarse-grind the coffee and add it to the Aeropress. Top up with water, then stir well after 30 seconds. Allow to brew for a further 2 minutes, then gently press the liquid through the filter. Allow it to cool. This recipe makes approximately 210 g of brewed coffee.

# BUYING GUIDE

## BRANDY

HENNESSY The biggest house in Cognac is the biggest for a reason. The full range of age statements for a full range of budgets. For me, you cannot go wrong with the Fine de Cognac and XO expressions. Great value for money.

LA DIABLADA Pisco is a hugely unrecognised category and one worthy of exploration. I love La Diablada, as it combines fragrant, winey top notes with a kind of oily grape-must depth.

LAIRD'S When it comes to applejack, the options can seem a bit limited. Fortunately, that doesn't matter too much, since brands like Laird's taste downright delicious.

## VODKA

BELVEDERE Poland is the producer of some of the world's best vodkas and Belvedere is the flagship brand. Made from a base of rye, all of the spirits in the Belvedere range have a pleasant peppery spice to the them that manages to shine through in mixed drinks.

CHASE Potato vodka doesn't sound great on paper, but it sure as hell tastes great in your mouth. Chase was one of the first of the recent glut of craft distilleries to open in the UK and has set the benchmark ever since. Expect to find characteristics of buttery mashed potato in its vodka.

VESTAL Another Polish brand, but this time sourced from single estates and bottled in vintages. This is brand, owned by Willy Borrell, is leading the charge for vodka with character.

## GIN

PORTOBELLO ROAD The classic branding of Portobello Road is reflective of what's in the bottle. Juicy juniper, subtle spice and fresh, herbal zing.

SIPSMITH A London Dry Gin produced in London, with powerful juniper aromatics, undiluted with neutral spirits – it's rarer than you think, but Sipsmith has nailed it.

TANQUERAY There are about a million gin brands available in the world today (OK, that's an exaggeration but there are a lot) so it's sometimes difficult to separate the wheat from the chaff. Tanqueray is one of the dependable pillars of the gin world, with its classic juniper-driven flavour profile made from just four botanicals.

## WHISKY

BULLEIT BOURBON/RYE Bulleit's hip flask-style bottle gives it the look of a brand that's been around for centuries. It hasn't, but that doesn't get away from the fact that this is delicious bourbon whisky, with a high rye content mash bill that adds spice and depth to cocktails.

CRAIGELLACHIE This Speyside malt is one of my favourite whiskies to mix with. It has tropical fruit characteristics as well as a rich meatiness that really stands up well in cocktails, while being a damn fine drink by itself.

DEWAR'S Blended whisky is born to be mixed with, and few blends have the versatility of Dewar's, which epitomises all those wonderful honeyed cereal and soft stone-fruit qualities that Scotch is famous for.

## TEQUILA & MEZCAL

DON JULIO There's enormous diversity in agave spirits, and I think the Don Julio range manages to encapsulate that, whether it's the pepper and salinity of the blanco, the stewed-apple fragrance of the reposado or the green tomato zing of the añejo.

OCHO A brand owned by one of the biggest names in tequila – Tomas Estes. Some great single-estate options that highlight terroir in agave.

SANTO DE PIEDRA This mescal has plenty of stone-fruit notes that complement a more subtle smoke character than you find in most mescal. Looks nice too.

# EQUIPMENT & SUPPLIERS

## GENERAL EQUIPMENT & GLASSWARE

**Cocktail Kingdom** Supplier of quality bar equipment – Yarai mixing beakers, Gallone mixing glasses, all manner of cobbler and Parisienne shakers, jiggers, strainers and kit bags. Reprints of vintage cocktail books are really good.
**www.cocktailkingdom.com**

**Drinkshop** General glassware and cocktail equipment – absinthe fountains, large selection of glassware and basic equipment.
**www.drinkshop.com**

**eBay** Seems like an obvious one, but I'm often impressed by the bargains that can be found on eBay, particularly where weird replacement parts for expensive machines are concerned.
**www.ebay.co.uk/.com**

**WMF** Reliable German kitchen equipment – pressure cookers, pans, utensils.
**www.wmf.com**

**Fisher Scientific** (UK) One-stop shop for lab equipment and sundries.
**www.fisher.co.uk**

**Chef Steps** (US) Sous vide, handheld smokers, scales and thermometers.
**store.chefsteps.com**

## SPECIALIST INGREDIENTS

**MSK Ingredients** Large range of own-brand powdered flavours, gelling agents and emulsifiers.
**www.msk-ingredients.com**

**Infusions 4 Chefs** Specialist ingredients, equipment and serviceware. Stockist of Texturas, Mugaritz, Lyo and Sosa ranges of products.
**www.infusions4chefs.co.uk**

**Cream Supplies** (UK) Molecular gastronomy ingredients. Cuisine Innovation and Kalys branded products.
**www.creamsupplies.co.uk**

**BrewUK** (UK) Home-brew suppliers – sterilisation, containers, filters, yeast, ingredients, bottles.
**www.brewuk.co.uk**

**Witchcraft Shop** (UK) Unexpected supplier of a vast range of quality dried herbs, spices, flowers, roots and barks (including cinchona bark).
**www.witchcraftshop.co.uk**

**Baldwins** (UK) Long-time purveyors of ingredients, tinctures and infusions.
**www.baldwins.co.uk**

**Modernist Pantry** (US) Full range of modernist ingredients for all manner of applications.
**www.modernistpantry.com**

**Terra Spice Company** (US) Vast range of dried fruits and spices, as well as specialist ingredients and powders for modernist applications.
**www.terraspice.com**

## SPECIALIST EQUIPMENT

**Amazon** While I'd urge you to spend your money in smaller, more independent stores where you can, Amazon surprises me on an almost daily basis with its ability to stock/source just about anything.
**www.amazon.co.uk/.com**

**KitchenAid** The classic food mixer. Useful for ice creams, sorbets and emulsions.
**www.kitchenaid.com**

**Buchi** The original rotary evaporator manufacturer – also chillers and vacuum pumps. Lots of other specialist lab equipment.
**www.buchi.com**

**Thermomix** Jack-of-all-trades food mixer, used for blending, emulsifying, infusing, heating and much more besides.
**www.thermomix.com**

**Polyscience** High-end professional kitchen technology – sous vide, food smokers, rotary evaporators.
**www.polyscience.com**

**Cream Supplies** (UK) Molecular gastronomy gadgets. Cream whippers, soda syphons, lab beakers, scales, smoking gun, magnetic stirrers, sous vide, sundries.
**www.creamsupplies.co.uk**

**Polybags** (UK) Good-value supplier of many types of bag, including all kinds of sous vide applications.
**www.polybags.co.uk**

**Cheftools** (UK) Supplier of Pacojet (ice cream and sorbet mixer), sous vide, smokers and Superbags (for filtering).
**www.cheftools.co.uk**

# GLOSSARY

**ABSORPTION** Process of a solid, liquid or gas being 'taken in' by another solid, liquid or gas.

**ACETONE** A flavourful ketone produced during the fermentation process.

**ACID PHOSPHATE** A traditional mixture of phosphoric acid and mineral salts of magnesium, potassium and calcium. Commonly used as a soda souring agent in early-20th-century America.

**ADSORPTION** Adhesion of particles to a surface. Principal mechanism of charcoal filtration.

**AGAR** Gelling agent (hydrocolloid) derived from red seaweed. Used for creating heat-stable gels and for clarification. Typical usage: 0.5–2 per cent.

**AGAVE** Thick, fibrous plant, the heart (or piña) of which is cooked and used to make tequila.

**ALBUMIN** Egg-white protein, used for stabilising foams, airs and in place of egg white in cocktails that call for it. Always mix with water before using.

**ATOMISE** A spritzed or sprayed aroma, usually directed at glassware or the surface of a drink.

**BAR** (measurement) Air pressure equal to 14.5 psi and 1000 mbar.

**BOTANICAL** Fruit, herb, flower or spice used to flavour gin during distillation process.

**BRIX** Measurement of sugar present within a solution, syrup, product or infusion. 50 brix is equivalent to 50 per cent of the total weight of the product comprising sugar.

**CASE-HARDENING** The phenomenon of a product's exterior surface drying during dehydration, slowing the migration of moisture from the interior of the product (*see* page 42).

**CITRIC ACID** Acid found in lemons and other citrus fruit (*see* page 36).

**COLUMN STILL** Large distillation apparatus that rectifies a wash into <96 per cent spirit. Unusually uses steam and bubble plates in a continuous process.

**CONTINUOUS STILL** *see* column still.

**CUTTING** (spirits production) The act of separating sections of a distillate for the purpose of quality and maintaining a high alcohol by volume (ABV).

**DISTILLATION** Process of separating alcohol and/or other volatile compounds out of a mixture based on their boiling points. Controlled through heat and air pressure.

**DRY ICE** Carbon dioxide ($CO_2$) in solid state. Temperature is approx. -79°C/-110.2°F. Sublimates into gas and can be used for a variety of applications (*see* page 59).

**ETHANOL** (ethyl alcohol) Flavourless and colourless alcohol found in all spirits and liqueurs. Has a boiling point of 78.3°C/172.9°F and a freezing point of -114°C/-173°F.

**EMULSION** Opaque, stable mixture of water and fat.

**FERMENTATION** Conversion of carbohydrates to alcohol (ethanol)/organic acids, heat and $CO_2$ through a microbiological organism.

**FRUCTOSE** Fruit-derived sugar, approx. 1.6 times sweeter than sucrose.

**FUSEL OILS** Generic term describing heavy (high-boiling-point) alcohols produced during fermentation that add characterful, deep flavours to distillations.

**GELATIN** Collagen-based gelling agent, usually derived from fish or pig skins. Check bloom strength and adjust according to the texture you want.

**GELLAN** Carbohydrate-based gelling agent. Great for making fluid gels and brittle jellies. Comes in two varieties: low acyl and high acyl.

**GLUCOSE** Very simple sugar, approximately 0.6 times the sweetness of sucrose.

**Gum Arabic** Derived from the sap of the acacia tree. Useful for oil-in-water emulsions such as those in soft drinks; also decreases surface tension and improves fizz in soft drinks.

**Heat of Fusion** Energy (joules) required to convert 1 g ice into 1 g of water – also applicable to other elements and compounds (*see* page 28).

**Ketone** Organic, often flavour-providing compound

**Kombucha** Fermented sweet tea

**Lecithin** Phospholipid-based emulsifier found in egg yolks. Used for creating airs and foams and for stabilising fat in water solutions. Typically used in levels of 0.1–1 percent. Commonly available unbranded or as Lecite from the Texturas range.

**Lignin** Compound present in plants and wood that makes up part of secondary plant cell structure. Responsible for much of the aromatic compounds produced when wood is charred or burned and also a big player in the realms of barrel ageing (*see* page 53).

**Liquid Nitrogen** (LN$_2$) Nitrogen in liquid form at approx -196°C. Used for a variety of chilling applications (*see* page 49).

**Malic Acid** Acid particularly prevalent in green apples. More tart than citric acid with a longer flavour.

**Methanol** Volatile light alcohol produced in small quantities during fermentation. Toxic when consumed in large quantities.

**Nitrogen** *See* liquid nitrogen.

**Nitrogen Cavitation** Describes the sudden and violent effervescence of nitrogen bubbles in a liquid. Used to speed up infusion times (*see* pages 38–9).

**Nitrous Oxide** (N$_2$O) Gas used for pressurising a cream whipper.

**Nucleation Site** Localised formation of bubbles dissolved in a gaseous liquid, for example bubbles appearing on the inside of a Champagne flute.

**Pot Still** Traditional kettle-style still.

**Rotary Evaporator** (rotavap) Low-pressure distillation apparatus. Facilitates distillation of liquids at low temperatures (< 40°C). Allows concentration and preservation of temperature-sensitive ingredients.

**Salinity** The proportion of salt present within a liquid, solution or product.

**Shrub** Preservation of fruit in either vinegar or alcohol. A method of infusing flavour into vinegars for use in cocktails.

**Sous Vide** (under vacuum) Practice describing both the sealing of ingredients in a plastic pouch and heating/cooking of ingredients in a water bath. Very useful for controlled concentration of aromatics in alcoholic and non-alcoholic infusions.

**Specific Heat** Energy required (joules) to heat 1 g of a material by 1°C.

**Sublimation** Transition of a substance directly from a solid to a gas (skipping the liquid phase) – most notably in dry ice.

**Sucrose** A simple sugar comprising a fructose molecule bonded to a glucose molecule. Usually derived from sugar cane or sugar beet.

**Sugar Syrup** (2:1) To make about 1 litre of sugar syrup, take 660 g caster (sucrose) sugar and gently heat with 264 g water and 66 g vodka. Once all the sugar has dissolved, bottle it and pop it in the fridge for up to 6 months.

**Tartaric Acid** Grape acid. Tart and short-lived.

**Vanilla Gomme Syrup** To make, split a whole vanilla pod/bean lengthways, scrape out the seeds, and gently heat with 300 g/10½ oz. caster/superfine sugar and 150 ml/5 fl. oz. water (makes approx. 450 ml/ 15 fl. oz.)

**Volatile** (aroma) An aromatic molecule with a high-vapour pressure that will quickly evaporate or sublimate into the surrounding air.

**Xanthan Gum** Polysaccharide of bacterial origin. Useful for gelling and thickening liquids without the need for heat.

# INDEX

# ACKNOWLEDGMENTS

As always, the biggest thanks of all must go to my family (Laura, Dexter, Robin) for allowing me to lock myself away in a dark room with a load of alcohol for six months.

Thanks to Addie, Sari and Matt for helping to make the drinks in this book look awesome. Thanks to Nathan for making the sentences in this book make perfect sense. Thanks, once again, to all of the team at RPS and beyond for placing reckless levels of trust in me: Cindy, David, Geoff, Julia, Leslie and Trish.

I'd also like to thank the following people, who have had ideas bounced off them, contributed a historical tidbit that has found its way in to this book, or just bought me a drink and sat with me while I drank it:

T. Aske, J. Burger, S. Calabrese, F. Campbell, R. Chetiyawardana, A. Dedianko, J. Fowler, A. Francis, I. Griffiths, D. Haldane, C. Harper, M. Helm, E. Holcroft, J. Kluger, F. Limon, E. Lorincz, D. Moncrieffe, D. McGuirk, S. Scott, C. Shannon, C. Warner, T. Solberg and B. Wilson.

# ABOUT THE AUTHOR

Tristan Stephenson is an award-winning bar operator, bartender, barista, chef, some-time journalist, drinks consultant and bestselling author of The Curious Bartender series of drinks books. In 2009 he was ranked 3rd in the UK Barista Championships. He was awarded UK bartender of the year in 2012 and in the same year was included in the London Evening Standard's 'Top 1000 most influential Londoners'. He has also been included in Drinks International's 'Bar World 100' in 2020, 2021 and 2022.

Having started his career in the kitchens of various Cornish restaurants, Tristan was eventually given the task of designing cocktails and running bar operations for Jamie Oliver's Fifteen restaurant (in Cornwall) back in 2007. He then went on to work for the world's biggest premium drinks company, Diageo, for two years.

After co-founding Fluid Movement in 2009, Tristan opened two bars in London – Purl, his first, in 2010, and then the Worship Street Whistling Shop in 2011. Worship Street Whistling Shop was awarded Time Out London's best new bar in 2011 and was placed in the 'World's Fifty Best Bars' for three consecutive years. In 2014 Fluid Movement opened their next venue, this time outside of London. Surfside, a steak and lobster restaurant on Polzeath beach in North Cornwall, was awarded the No. 1 Position in The Sunday Times's 'Best alfresco dining spots in the UK 2015'. In 2016 Fluid

Movement opened three new London bars on the same site in Shoreditch, most notably Black Rock (a bar dedicated to whisky) which became a four-time winner of UK's Best Specialist Bar award. A second Black Rock arrived in Bristol in 2019, and a third in Shanghai, China, in 2021.

Tristan's first book, The Curious Bartender: The Artistry & Alchemy of Creating the Perfect Cocktail was published in October 2013 and shortlisted for the prestigious André Simon Award. His second book, The Curious Bartender: An Odyssey of Malt, Bourbon & Rye Whiskies hit the bookshelves in October 2014. In Spring 2015 he published The Curious Barista's Guide to Coffee (having previously successfully harvested, processed, roasted and brewed the first cup of UK-grown coffee from the Eden Project in Cornwall, achieving international press coverage).

His fourth book The Curious Bartender's Gin Palace, was again shortlisted for the André Simon Award. During the course of this research for this project, Tristan travelled to over 150 distilleries around the world, in over 20 countries, including Scotland, Mexico, Cuba, France, Lebanon, Italy, Guatemala, Japan, the US and Spain.

Next, his fifth book The Curious Bartender's Rum Revolution was published in 2017 and involved a tour that demonstrated how rum has moved beyond its Caribbean heartlands, with vibrant new distilleries appearing in Brazil, Venezuela, Colombia and Guatemala and in unexpected corners of the world, from Australia to Mauritius and from the Netherlands to Japan.

This, his sixth book was originally published by Ryland Peters & Small in 2018 as The Curious Bartender (Volume II): The New Testament of Cocktails, and is a follow-up to the original bestselling book The Curious Bartender (Volume 1): The Artistry & Alchemy of Creating the Perfect Cocktail.

Tristan's other commercial enterprises to date have included drinks brand Aske-Stephenson, which manufactured and sold pre-bottled cocktails in flavours as diverse as Peanut Butter and Jam Old-Fashioned and Flat White Russian. He also launched an on-line whisky subscription service called whisky-me.com (as seen on BBC TV's Dragon's Den), which enables customers to receive single malt whiskies for home delivery. In 2017 Tristan joined supermarket chain Lidl UK as a consultant on their own-brand spirits range. He also hosts the Diageo Bar Academy podcast Bar Chat.

Tristan lives in Cornwall and is husband to Laura and father to two small children. In his very limited spare time he runs (a lot), rides a Triumph motorcycle, takes photos, designs websites, cooks stuff, attempts various DIY tasks beyond his level of ability and collects whisky and books.